PREPARING THE GROUND
discovering the everyday practices of design

Kendall Hunt
publishing company

Randall Teal
University of Idaho

Cover image by Randall Teal

Kendall Hunt
publishing company

www.kendallhunt.com
Send all inquiries to:
4050 Westmark Drive
Dubuque, IA 52004-1840

Copyright © 2012 by Kendall Hunt Publishing Company

ISBN 978-1-4652-2730-0

Printed in the United States of America
10 9 8 7 6 5 4

CONTENTS

Principles of Design

CONTENTS

PREPARING THE GROUND
discovering the everyday practices of design

context **of design**

"L'Hôpital Saint-Paul à Saint-Rémy," Vincent Van Gogh.

why art and design
MATTER

"I tell you: one must still have chaos within oneself, to give birth to a dancing star."[1]
Friedrich Nietzsche

We live in a world that is becoming increasingly homogeneous and predictable. Education in particular constantly attempts to overcome the chaos of irregular processes and unmeasurable outcomes by standardizing its methods and metrics. In this flawed system, most students come to think that memorization equals knowledge, facts equal truth, and thinking is a mere retrieval of factual data. Unfortunately, such a focus on the measurable, unambiguous, and reproducible in education leads to a fundamental diminishment of our human capacity for thought—thought that should be nuanced, multifaceted, and not focused on reductive tasks.

When reductive thinking takes over, we tend to forget that the complexities of life are the very substance of life. In other words, the more we imagine that mastering chaos is our job as human beings, the more we move to eliminate the intricate relationships and interactions that so enrich the experience of life. This is perhaps why the South African architect Jo Noero said that designers should not think of themselves as problem solvers, but instead should think of themselves as visionaries.[2] What he means to communicate here is that mere problem solving tends to strip experiences

An additive process is a way of making that operates by assembling smaller parts into a larger whole. Collage works on additive principles. Additive also can generally refer to a work that expresses the fact that it has been made of several components. Examples like these are said to have an additive form.

ADDITIVE

of their richness, and instead of making reductive solutions, designers should always seek to elevate experiences and the particular richness of life through their creative interventions. The practices of art and creativity facilitate such an elevation.

The practices of art and creativity lie at the base of the design disciplines and thrive upon the very complexities that our reductive modes of thought attempt to eliminate. Unfortunately, many students have been trained by our educational systems and cultural institutions to see art as a kind of frivolous pursuit. Maybe they see it as a pastime that's charming, even astonishing —but still one that is mostly irrelevant to any kind of a practical engagement with life. After all, art is merely the ability to make lifelike or beautiful things, right? While these definitions might be true for a given incidence of art, to imagine that these narrow notions of art are definitive would be misguided.

Although such characterizations are not quite fair because they present a caricatured misunderstanding of art, they do serve as useful provocations, because they are unfortunately close to the views shared by many who imagine artists to be irresponsible dreamers who have no real-world skills. In fact, Florida Governor Rick Scott recently passed just such a judgment on all of the liberal arts, saying, in essence, that they were irrelevant to any kind of real-world activities and that those majoring in liberal arts were thus unemployable.[3] Such ignorance and misrepresentation are among the greatest challenges that art and education in general have to face, because they reinforce the tendency to measure the effectiveness of education by the success one has in finding immediate employment in a chosen field, rather than how that education has helped to enhance one's ability for critical thought and effective action and thus enhanced one's potential for future success.

This limited view of education is indicative of a more general limitation in the way we think. That is, we tend to assume linear one-to-one relationships within a system that is neither linear nor one-to-one. In other words, life is changeable and characterized by contingent and unpredictable events, and more often than not, plays out in ways that are different than what we imagined might happen. Or, as former Beatle John Lennon once said, "Life is what happens to you while you're busy making

An additive process of making and its resulting form.

principles of design

other plans."[4] Despite the obviousness of this fact, we frequently deny it because it makes us feel safe; yet, ironically, this "safety" decreases our ability to respond effectively to life's challenges and opportunities. The philosopher Friedrich Nietzsche claimed, "Only by forgetting that he himself is an artistically creating subject, does man live with any repose, security, and consistency."[5] Here, we see Nietzsche pointing to the human tendency to freeze the dynamics of life, because of the repose and comfort such freezing offers; yet in so doing we deny a fundamental aspect of our being—the creative.

As you will see throughout this book, art is not safe and it does not "work" in such a tidy linear fashion, and this is why it is such an important antidote to more shallow forms of thought. Instead of clarity, comfort, and safety, art demands ambiguity, unpredictability, and risk. When we learn the practices and methodologies that allow us to be creative, we take the first step in overcoming the reductive drives of our culture and its institutions. By learning to be more creative, it is possible to become deeply sensitive to the potency of our daily interactions. As artists and designers, this means not only that we become better thinkers, but we also become better able to produce solutions that have *vision*.

In short, your basic design training will tell you that, memorization *does not* equal knowledge, facts *do not* equal truth, and thinking is *much more than* a mere retrieval of factual data. Here, we will discover that true thinking requires immersion, exploration, experimentation, questioning, making things, and above all sensitivity to the world around us.

a case for
DYNAMIC EDUCATION

"When the laws of mathematics refer to reality, they are not certain. And when they are certain, they do not refer to reality."[6]
Albert Einstein

Many introductory courses across disciplines begin by breaking down the discipline's complexity into its constituent parts. In so doing, these "foundation" courses aim to slowly build the parts back into the whole of the discipline. Although this approach might make some things easier to grasp, it has a tendency to miss the basic questions of significance and meaning that should structure the goals of

6

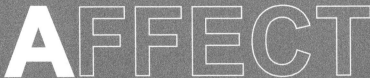

To create an effect or feeling. In art and design, affect addresses the way that art touches us on a sensory and emotional level.

AFFECT

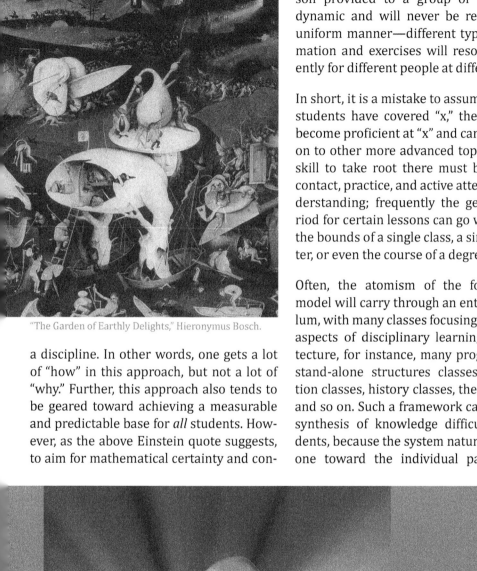

"The Garden of Earthly Delights," Hieronymus Bosch.

sistency is to not deal with reality. Unlike a building's foundation that is necessarily solid, static, uniform, and calculated, a lesson provided to a group of students is dynamic and will never be received in a uniform manner—different types of information and exercises will resonate differently for different people at different times.

In short, it is a mistake to assume that once students have covered "x," they will have become proficient at "x" and can then move on to other more advanced topics. For any skill to take root there must be repeated contact, practice, and active attempts at understanding; frequently the gestation period for certain lessons can go well beyond the bounds of a single class, a single semester, or even the course of a degree.

Often, the atomism of the foundational model will carry through an entire curriculum, with many classes focusing on discreet aspects of disciplinary learning. In architecture, for instance, many programs have stand-alone structures classes, construction classes, history classes, theory classes, and so on. Such a framework can make the synthesis of knowledge difficult for students, because the system naturally orients one toward the individual parts of the

a discipline. In other words, one gets a lot of "how" in this approach, but not a lot of "why." Further, this approach also tends to be geared toward achieving a measurable and predictable base for *all* students. However, as the above Einstein quote suggests, to aim for mathematical certainty and con-

principles of design

Moby: music, too, affects us.

Building Foundation, Seattle, Washington.

shift and clutch, eventually discovering how to manipulate gas and brake pedals, and ultimately combining a mastery in each of these areas into "driving." Instead, one learns to drive by driving, which by definition involves a simultaneous interrelation and operation of its various parts. The German philosopher Martin Heidegger gives this idea a punchy spin saying, "We shall never learn what is called swimming . . . by reading a treatise on swimming. Only a leap into the river tells us what is called swimming."[7] In short, we practice synthetic understanding in many aspects of our lives, but it often escapes us when it comes to more complicated situations—situations where it matters most. There is an excellent passage in *Moby Dick* where Herman Melville describes the kind of complexity that can be grasped only through experience. He says:

> . . . it may be fancied, that from the naked skeleton of the stranded whale, accurate hints may be derived touching his true form. Not at all . . . the great Leviathan is that one creature in the world which must remain unpainted to the last. True, one portrait may hit the mark much nearer than another, but none can hit it with any very considerable degree of ex-

discipline, often obscuring of the dynamic whole. Although there are times when an intensity of focus on an isolated part can be helpful, there is also the danger that the seductiveness of such focus will obfuscate the need for orchestration and assimilation on the part of the designer. Critically, it is exactly this kind of dynamic integration that designers will be asked to practice in the real world.

Interestingly, the importance of synthesis seems to be obvious in other parts of our lives. For example, we understand that it would be difficult to learn how to drive by first learning how to turn a wheel, then studying the finer points of using a stick

An array occurs when three or more elements are laid out in a pattern. This is a useful technique for creating continuity without making elements conjoined.

actness. So there is no earthly way of finding out precisely what the whale really looks like. And the only mode in which you can derive even a tolerable idea of his living contour, is by going a whaling yourself; but by so doing, you run no small risk of being eternally stove and sunk by him. Wherefore, it seems to me you had best not be too fastidious in your curiosity touching this Leviathan.[8]

So, for both Heidegger and Melville, it is not only that these involved aspects of meaning not be overlooked: the important thing is that they are perhaps more meaningful than other understandings. Striving for definitive understanding always places one on the verge of crossing a line where clarity destroys the mystery of meaning.

Art and design are filled with encounters and problems that dwell exactly in this realm. And, unfortunately, when students become uncomfortable with such overlapping forces and the type of integrated thought necessary for properly relating to them, they will frequently eliminate large areas of concern just to manage a given problem. This, of course, leads to major problems: oversights, simplifications, neglected resources, inappropriate interventions, and so on. This point brings us to a principal tenet of this book—that synthesis is one of the most critical yet difficult things for young designers to become skilled at, and therefore it should be central to their basic design education. Further, this synthesis of knowledge must ultimately exceed one's discipline. On this point, architect Michael Sorkin has argued that undergraduate architecture programs often function as "formulae for fundamental literacy" spending too much time "learning structures and CAD" and not enough on "Shakespeare, Oceanic art, or *The Tale of Genji*" (Sorkin 2009, 34). Here, Sorkin highlights the need for a more worldly knowledge—that is, *knowledge that makes connections* between one's discipline and the bigger issues of being human. Educators Earnest Boyer and Lee Mitgang add some depth to Sorkin's comment:

In a rapidly changing world, students need to be able to look beyond the confines of a single discipline and view problems in their totality. To understand the ethical choices entailed in any profession, students should be exposed to how the great figures in history, literature, philosophy and art have struggled with life's moral dilemmas.[9]

An array of Torii gates at Inari Shrine, Kyoto, Japan.

principles of design

To have encountered and thought about Hamlet or Doctor Faustus in literature, or to have read Hobbes and Rousseau in philosophy, and even to weigh the words of history's most notorious architect, Albert Speer, are experiences of incalculable value to anyone engaged in professional study.[10]

Although both of these comments were made specific to architectural education, the point is more generally applicable to the practice of design, and therefore vital for young designers to understand. The reason these comments are vital is that designers are always tasked with designing things that should connect to and enhance the lives and very existence of others and their place in the world. Therefore, it is critical that designers have familiarity with, and ultimately some expertise in, things like life, beauty, society, economics, ecology, emotions, the acquisition of knowledge, and so on.

With this goal of diversity of knowledge in mind, the information and ideas contained in this book are interdisciplinary in nature and are designed to make you think. The latter is done, in part, to encourage the idea that thinking is an *active* state that facili-

tates the intake of knowledge. That is, the material cannot be passively absorbed or memorized, but rather must be engaged with the intent of discovering meaning and significance. In order to do this, this book will ask you to pursue connections between conceptual, theoretical, and historical ideas, and try to make links to this material and your own design work. The hope is that in doing this, you will begin to formulate ideas about the ways in which art and design can positively affect society and our lives as human beings, and how you can use the understanding gleaned from such reflection to strengthen the impact of your own work. Ultimately, practicing this kind of thinking and interactive processing will better prepare you for the complex world you will ultimately design for; when complexity can be engaged as such through design, the final products will be more attuned, nuanced, and appropriate.

toward a design
ECOLOGY

"Water that is clear has no fish."[11]
Ts'ai ken t'an

The ability to navigate and synthesize complexity should be thought of as one of the designer's fundamental skills. Unfor-

A state of unbalance, where elements in one area of the composition are different than those on the other side. Asymmetry can be a useful technique for creating a sense of dynamics and movement in your work.

ASYMMETRY

Glacier National Park Ecosystem.

tunately, this skill is frequently neglected in the foundational notion of basic design. So, in order to foster an ability for working with complexity and to further integrated thinking in design, perhaps it is better to imagine basic design education not as a *foundation*, but as an *ecosystem*. Foundations are fixed and unmoving, but ecosystems remain healthy through constant inputs of rain and sunlight and a diversity of flora and fauna. They undergo processes of growing and blossoming as well as violence, death, decay, and decomposition.

Using the metaphor of an ecosystem to envision design is useful for several reasons. First, it associates design with a type of system that remains vital not despite, but because of its complexity and changeability. An ecosystem is as design education should

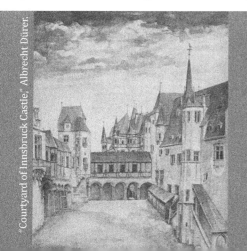

"Courtyard of Innsbruck Castle," Albrecht Dürer.

principles of design

be—a multifaceted, dynamic, self-perpetuating system that is always emerging and building upon itself and is never complete.

The second aspect of the ecosystem metaphor that is helpful is the ecosystem's dependence on soil. In healthy ecosystems, the ground is filled with nutrients, microflora, and microfauna that in turn support the growth and development of a diverse host of macroflora and macrofauna. We might imagine a basic design course as having an analogous composition. Then we could stop thinking of it as a static and impervious base upon which we might build later skills, and start thinking of it instead as a nutrient-filled soil that encourages the growth of a diverse ecology of abilities, principles, ideas, strategies, and perspectives. When we think of an introductory design course as an ecosystem, we get a course that at its core attempts to construct a medium within which many essential skills can take root. In other words, introductory design thought of as an ecosystem becomes a course that endeavors to make each student into a fertile ground, a productive site where various positions, skills, and specific inputs can grow up over the years.

Related to this last point, the third reason an ecosystem metaphor is useful is because it highlights the fact that many skills and concepts cannot be understood immediately; rather, they must be "planted," so that they might later emerge to be effectual. For example, intangible skills such as intuition and emotion, as well as less concrete phenomena like time, perception, and experience, are all basic to any artistic endeavor; yet, mastering such ephemera often re-

Double-loaded corridor, Pennsylvania State University.

A strong linear connection between two distinct points. An axis is an excellent method for establishing a relationship to a viewer, because its directness and clarity make it feel like the design addresses you directly.

Axes are often associated with symmetry, where an axis will often bisect a composition highlighting the equality of its respective sides. An axis coupled with symmetry provides a strong sense of center and balance.

AXIS

quires more practice and maturation than, say, understanding terms like point, line, and plane. Therefore, it is important that young artists engage both simple and sophisticated elements, principles, and ideas so that the latter have the time to mature. In short, more sophisticated concepts and skills demand even more patience, practice, and experience to become fully functional than the more straightforward principles and ideas—an acorn becomes an oak over many years, but it can only do so because it has been planted early enough to have the time to mature. So it is with many of the concepts in this book.

the problem of the
THINKING-I

"The suggestion is that the function of the brain and nervous system and sense organs is in the main eliminative and not productive."[12]
Aldous Huxley

We, as human beings, are very good at eliminating information in order to aid our functioning in the world. And certainly, this skill is very useful to numerous daily tasks. However, as the above quote suggests, Aldous Huxley was concerned that this filtering function of the brain hampered our creativity. Here, Huxley was on to something, as this aspect of our brains and a particular type of thinking associated with it are, in fact, the basis of our aforementioned desires to make things standardized and measurable. French philosopher Henri Bergson explained the role of our intellect this way:

> The essential function of our intellect, as the evolution of life has fashioned it, is to be a light for our conduct, to make ready for our action on things, to foresee, for a given situation, the events favorable or unfavorable, which may follow thereupon. Intellect therefore instinctively selects in a given situation whatever is like something already known; it seeks this out, in order that it might apply its principle that "like produces like."[13]

In short, the intellect prefers to make equations and shortcuts so that it might avoid having to face situations in their specificity, and our rational brains will do just about anything to achieve clarity and certainty. Yet, this discomfort with unpredictability was never extreme until the beginnings of modern science.

One of the founders of modern science was the French philosopher René Descartes.

Axis: Palace-de-Versailles, France.

principles of design

Descartes was an influential writer who was particularly unnerved by the uncertainty of the world. Descartes once claimed:

> I will suppose then, that everything I see is spurious. I will believe that my memory tells me lies, and that none of the things that it reports ever happened. I have no senses. Body, shape, extension, movement and place are chimeras. So what remains true? Perhaps just the one fact that nothing is certain.[14]

In response to his discomfort Descartes sought solace in his rational mind. The culmination of his search for certainty is summed up in his famous "*cogito ego sum*" —"I think therefore I am." In discovering the power and reassurance of the rational mind—what we will refer to as "the thinking-I"—Descartes believed he had come up with a solution to the "problem" of uncertainty. However, Descartes took this solution to an extreme. He describes his revelation:

> At last I have discovered it—thought; this alone is inseparable from me. I am, I exist—that is certain. But for how long? For as long as I am thinking. For it could be that were I totally to cease from thinking, I should totally cease to exist.[15]

In this statement Descartes is not simply suggesting, "I think therefore I am," but rather more problematically, "I am because I think." In other words, Descartes imagined that if he stopped thinking, he might, in fact, no longer exist! Instead of suffering that dubious fate, Descartes sought the reassurance and safety of a kind of thinking that relied on his being conscious of himself. Now imagine for a moment all of the things that you do that involve not being explicitly conscious of yourself: walking to school, driving in your car, playing sports, listening to music, watching movies, drawing, talking with a friend—the list could go on indefinitely. The point here is that in his revelation about the importance of being aware of the fact that you are thinking, Descartes devalued all sorts of different capacities for thought simply because they did not operate in a predictable and self-certain way. Further, by promoting what amounts to being self-conscious, Descartes was endorsing a disposition (self-consciousness) that we tend to equate with being timid, shy, and afraid. Not a very productive state.

Unfortunately, this fixation did not just remain Descartes's private obsession. The split that Descartes had initiated became deeply influential for many, and because of

An axonometric drawing is a particular type of three-dimensional drawing. As opposed to perspective drawings, which tend to give a subjective viewpoint (i.e., put the viewer in the scene), axonometric drawings generally provide an objective view of the project (i.e., seeing the project as an object). An axonometric drawing is characterized by lines that remain parallel to one another.

AXONOMETRIC

this, the thinking-I has had remarkable staying power. With the thinking-I, we inherit a world of questionable realities, senses that cannot be trusted, and an overestimation of the effects of human control upon the course of life. Ultimately, this particular self-conscious way of thinking has come to be the very definition of thinking, which has demoted sensory experience, intuition, and emotion to being lower forms of processing. With this shift, we became less sensitive to the subtleties of our daily interactions and, perhaps most importantly, ascribed importance to individual control in the process of thinking.

This last point is important because what grows out of this misconception is a human-centric notion world. Such a belief easily merged with a movement known as humanism, which is perhaps most succinctly summed up by the Greek philosopher Protagoras, who said, "Man is the measure of all things."[16] The problem with this view is that it causes us to overestimate our own singular importance in the creation of our lives (and our designs) and to treat everything else as resources for our unlimited use. This self-centeredness encourages designers to stop being responsive to the people, places, and problems that they should be designing for and thus leads us to severely deplete the assets of both the natural and lived worlds.

In short, the thinking–I overvalues itself as the font of all creativity, knowledge, and ideas, and will reduce the complexity and fluidity of the lived world in order to distract from the importance of external factors—other than one's mind—to the choices we might make and the things we can do. Paradoxically, the way to correct this deficiency is by reconnecting with ambiguity, because a feeling of ambiguity indicates that you are coping with the real complexity of a situation.

This is a basic challenge for the designer—to let ambiguity exist (and often persist) in design problems. That is, when you have a sense of the multitude of possibilities that are present in any design problem, you are designing in a way that is participatory (i.e., not controlling). Ironically, when you welcome uncertainty as a designer, you will feel a greater freedom to commit to your ideas, because you will recognize that a design is evolutionary and that any answer you might come up with is ultimately provisional (i.e., with this perspective there are no "bad" choices). In other words, design

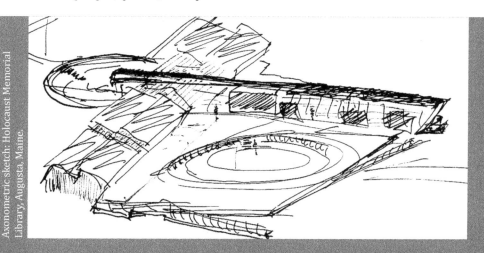

Axonometric sketch: Holocaust Memorial Library, Augusta, Maine.

principles of design

solutions are always subject to revision because the conditions or parameters of a design can change, either on their own or because you have come to understand them differently; and to see this means that you have begun to understand that design is a process, not a product. There is no 2+2 in design.

Design problems are like going to a restaurant that you have never been to; if you try to order based on what is objectively the best dish, chances are that you will stress yourself out as you try to make little arguments for each possible candidate for your dinner. Frequently, these internal debates lead to disappointing selections. Have you ever thought, "I wish I had ordered the ____"? Most of us have. So, something like dinner choice is not merely an objective proposition: "best" is codependent on a patron's tastes and level of hunger, the time of day, the time of year, a restaurant's specialty, who is cooking, and so on. Yet, becoming consciously aware of the multitude of factors that are going to play into your decision is not the solution—carefully weighing out all the factors and using them to make the "right" choice often leads to the aforementioned bad choice or to an inability to make a choice.

Here, the importance of those other intelligences that we as human beings possess— emotion, sensation, intuition—begins to become evident. Although we rely on our senses and feelings frequently (despite the prejudices of the thinking-I), we often become suspicious of them in more formal situations, situations where the decisions "matter." However, in the restaurant example, it is contrived, if not absurd, to arrive for dinner and attempt to scientifically choose the "right" thing, because more often than not our bodies tell us what they want immediately, and sometimes emphatically. Certainly, we must generally operate by adding a conscious deliberation to these feelings—"No, I can't have the cake because that will be fattening," "I am allergic to eggs," or "No, I won't have fish because we are having trout tomorrow night." However, rational thought should not initiate choice: it should be added to an impulse in order to filter or confirm what our body is already telling us. In short, sensory and emotional feedback is critical to making good choices. Here, it is useful to bear in mind that like begets like, which is to say that seeking something like emotion by way of the intellect will only bring an intellectualization of said emotion.

The simplest kind of balance is symmetrical balance, where the elements on one side of the composition are the same as the ones on the opposite. However, balance speaks more generally to a state of equilibrium in a work. Looking at work in terms of balance allows a means of creating harmony with elements that might otherwise be disparate.

BALANCE

Ultimately it is not a question of either/or when it comes to thinking, rational or a-rational: instead, it is a question of how to draw upon all of our capacities equally in order to synthesize vast amounts of information and retain its meaningful complexity. However, we must proceed as Aristotle once said, by:

> dragging ourselves over to the opposite side, for by pulling far away from going wrong we will come to the mean, the very thing that people do who straighten warped pieces of lumber.[17]

In other words, we must overpursue the abilities that have atrophied under the yoke of the thinking-I so that we might again become balanced in the way we think.

expanding the definition of
THINKING

"We can learn thinking only if we radically unlearn what thinking has been traditionally."[18]
Martin Heidegger

Sometimes decisions that are more informed by our a-rational abilities are referred to as "going with your gut." This phrase is a fine place to begin to imagine alternative intelligences; however, it is im-portant to demystify—or perhaps better, to enrich—this adage. There are two reasons for this "enrichment." The first is simply to demonstrate *why* such modes of thought are as legitimate as the measured and self-aware thinking we are used to. The second reason is even more important: we need to understand the depth and background of the processes at work when we "go with our gut," so that such abilities can be

"The Home Lesson," Albert Anker.

"Girl with a Broom," Rembrandt van Rijn.

There can also be more dynamic states of balance where the balance is not characterized by harmony, but by more charged relationships. See tension.

principles of design

practiced and enhanced and not just be thought of as arbitrary or mystical.

In order to develop additional intelligences, one must first understand one's own capacities. In a book called the *Nicomachean Ethics*, Aristotle laid out a critical group of five capacities specifically related to the way we think. These different modes of thinking are *techne* (art), *episteme* (knowledge), *nous* (intellect), *phronesis* (practical wisdom), and *sophia* (wisdom). Aristotle's effort to dissect the ways that we process and engage information is useful in the context of design, because it makes explicit the different potentials we have for processing, learning, and acting within the world. Here, it is important to note that although these categories are made explicit as a means of better understanding them, ultimately one does not simply choose one mode of operating over another; rather, these faculties work together in concert and complement one another constantly if we develop the habits to facilitate their vitality.

Aristotle's definitions (in italics) orient us to the capacities for thought that the successful designer must possess. To begin with, a designer must have a knowledge base—*episteme*—to draw from when faced with possibilities and decisions. This includes such things as knowledge of historic design precedents, disciplinary terminology, basic principles and skills, ideas about

"Aristotle Contemplating the Bust of Homer," Rembrandt van Rijn.

A cliché occurs in design when we turn to hackneyed responses, when we rely upon phrases, ideas, and visuals that are overly familiar. When clichés enter our work, it lacks rigor and emotion and leads us to caricatures instead of work with substance. A cliché can be anything from a phrase like "going with your gut" to using an image of an hourglass in a work that deals with time. In either case, the real

CLICHÉ

how to engage a design problem, and a knowledge of design tools and media. A designer must also be able to recognize the big picture of any design problem—*nous*—so that they can understand what is at stake and what matters in a given situation. For example, if faced with remodeling a house, it is critical to be able to recognize the potential that the existing house offers so that one does not obliterate it in the process of improving it. Otherwise, you might as well have started from scratch. It is the designer's job to see potential so that they might build upon it. This recognition of the whole is *nous*.

A third category—*phronesis*—speaks to the fact that one must be able to practically proceed, making choices, in a given context. *Phronesis* is that skill for *utilizing* relevant information, given stimuli, and acquired knowledge effectively. For example, you must learn to know when certain preliminary stages of a design are done so that you can move forward in development, you must learn when to call in outside experts (engineers, say), and you must learn to make choices about the proper media for a given design task (a canvas versus a piece of plywood, let's say). *Phronesis* is an aptitude for practical action. It is not about making things: it is about making choices and acting on them.

A fourth type of knowledge—*techne*—tells designers that they must have specific skill in producing things. *Techne* goes beyond mere manual skills and suggests that artists and designers must learn to see what is possible in a given material and be able to draw out and form these possibilities. Here, *techne* might be thought of as a producing that arises out of attentive listening. Regarding *techne* in cabinetmaking, Heidegger explains:

> If he is to become a true cabinetmaker, he makes himself answer and respond above all to the different kinds of wood and to the shapes slumbering within wood—to wood as it enters man's dwelling with all the hidden riches of its nature. In fact this relatedness to wood is what maintains the whole craft.[19]

Such skill should pervade the practices of art, and since *techne* directly ties thinking to making, we will discuss *techne* more later on.

Teamwork: a visual cliché.

depth of the idea is lost in the generality of the cliché. If you find yourself with a cliché, it means you need to go deeper, be more articulate, and push your work farther.

principles of design

A modern bathroom vanity cabinet.

and drive their particular field of inquiry. For example, "Why is art relevant today?" or "What are basic urban problems that trouble our cities and how do we begin to address them?" It is the contemplation of such issues that drives art and design to positive growth and altruistic ends, and it is being able to think clearly and speak wisely about such big questions that moves one from being a mere producer into a place where they might be seen as a mentor, expert, or visionary.

Aristotle's categories highlight the importance of not falling into the safety of one type of knowledge alone. For example, if one treated art as merely the ability to effectively render a likeness, then whole realms of exploration and discovery would be destroyed. Here you would miss out on the usefulness that a knowledge of history and principles can bring to your work; how an ability to translate ephemeral things (like the personality of someone sitting for a portrait) allows art to thrive; the ways that a skill in deliberation can aid your ability to adeptly choose subjects, media, and contexts for your work; and the ways in which the depth of artistic pursuits benefits from a reflective contemplation of life,

The fifth category encompasses the kind of knowledge we refer to as wisdom, or as Aristotle calls it, *sophia*. For the designer, *sophia* indicates that one must eventually engage their chosen discipline in terms of the bigger issues that influence, trouble,

A gestalt phenomenon that describes how one's mind will "finish" a shape based on the suggestion of several ambiguous marks. Closure relates to the effectiveness of arrays, in that our minds give them contiguity.

Closure might also be thought about more metaphorically in design. This occurs when a design offers us some ambiguity, thus asking us to "finish" it. Whether a shape or an idea, closure works on the same principle as a detective novel. In the

CLOSURE

humanity, and the qualities and issues that deliver significance to the situations that we encounter.

In short, what Aristotle's categories show us is that it would be pure folly to imagine our capacity for thought as a narrow and highly defined activity. This is why the concept of "habits of excellence" is so important. As we have seen, skills like drawing have certain cognitive principles that can be intellectualized, but ultimately work best when the principles no longer need to be thought about and one can just draw. In fact, having to think about techniques and principles generally becomes an obstacle very quickly. Just like one who is proficient in a sport or with a musical instrument, designers want to develop their knowledge and skills to a point where all exist in a state of cohesion and fluidity, where the embodiment of basic techniques and principles allows them to focus more intently on the work they are doing.

The other thing we learn from Aristotle's categories is that these different types of thinking necessarily overlap one another. That is, when all of our capacities work in harmony, our work will shine.

"Until we realize the unity of life we live in Fear."[20]
Upanishads

Overturning the drives of the thinking-I and activating our great range of other intelligences begins with seeing the vitality and, paradoxically, the unity that complexity brings to our experiences. Touching upon this very notion, the Greek philosopher Heraclitus once said, "You cannot step in the same river twice."[21] This is a deceptively simple description of an extremely rich phenomenon. What Heraclitus intends in this statement is that there is this thing that as a whole we call a river, yet the very thing that allows it to be defined as a river is its ever-changing flow of water. That is, its variability is its identity. Heraclitus meant this statement as an aphorism— something that was more generally true about life. So this idea would also apply to, say, a history course you are taking. Every other day you might attend this class called History of Western Civilization—it has a clear and identifiable identity in your mind and in the course catalogue. But if the class weren't different every time you came back

We tend to see these three dots as a triangle.

latter, there are just enough clues present for the outsider to feel like they can (and should) participate in trying to solve the crime. When design asks the viewer/user to finish what it has offered, it rewards them for their participation by making them feel smart—"I get it!"—and often design will feel richer because of this technique.

principles of design

to it, it would be boring, to say the least. Further, it's not the *label* of the course that makes it meaningful—what's important is the particular way that the teacher describes the specific events, people, places, and things and their implications. The whole of the Roman Empire, for example, is significant, because of the particular people, events, and accomplishments that make it up; and yet we need a notion of the Roman Empire to make coherent which interactions and relationships count as significant and why.

So it is that life's content and vitality reside in the reactions that occur between specific differences, and the wholes that we discern as a result of these interactions. Let us look at an everyday example, a conversation, in order to further clarify this concept. A conversation depends upon on both definition and a fundamental ambiguity, in that a pre-scripted conversation would not be a conversation; yet a conversation between participants that do not know how to have a conversation would not qualify as a conversation either. In other words, conversations occur spontaneously when we have both the whole—we are culturally familiarized with what conversations are—and the unique interacting parts that make them meaningful. Such an intertwined system runs counter to the thinking-I's desires for clarity, categories, and resolution, and it shows that labels and identities only remain vital and meaningful if there is this interplay and changeability at work. That is, a *living* identity must remain uncertain and ambiguous, because "living" means to be subject to the forces of time and change.

Like Heraclitus, the German philosopher Martin Heidegger believed that time and change were at the very heart of existence, and that the search for certainty severely limited the possibilities of life. With this in mind, he went so far as to suggest that a vital exchange with the world we inhabit can only occur though a primary encounter with nothingness—in our terms, living *with* ambiguity—because the experience of such uncertainly tempers the reductive tendencies of the rational mind. For Heidegger, process and involvement were critical to this tempering action. Here, Heidegger is observing the way that active involvement connects us to a situation at a precognitive level: that is, *before we become aware of the fact that we are thinking*. This is an important point and a crucial difference from the self-consciousness of the thinking-I.

The thing that Heidegger sees in our precognitive intelligences is that, unlike simplifications of the thinking-I, they provide the ground from which we can *engage* the unfamiliar, not eliminate it. This occurs because we have a capacity for embodied knowledge, which is knowledge that comes through continual practice. An accomplished athlete performing at the height of their ability is a perfect example of this kind of knowledge. However, this kind of knowledge is not limited to sports. For example, think about reading a book. Over time, you developed the ability to read, and now when you sit down with a book, you can focus on the content of the text instead of having to trouble over how to read, what words are, or how grammar works. So, the embodied knowledge that you possess about language and the act of reading allows you to penetrate through the surface of a text and move into that which is unfamiliar, namely its meaning.

23

"Garden Restaurant," August Macke.

A type of making that involves using scraps of materials and assembling them according to their unfiltered material state. Collage can be a very useful way of loosening up, because it operates from scraps. That is, the scraps of collage eliminate the need for you, as the artist, to make choices about the line you are drawing, parts you are creating, shape you are sculpting. In short, collage is an effective means of activating your intuitive thinking.

P.S.: When doing collage, do not think symbolically (i.e., collecting images that refer to something else); rather, think materially (i.e., color, texture, form, etc.) and in terms of affect.

COLLAGE

For designers it is important to remember that the everyday context is always "working" in this way, because this recognition begins to reconnect us to the real complexity of our experiences; for example, it is the confluence of food, atmosphere, service, price, company, and behavior of other diners that influences our feelings about whether a meal at a restaurant was a satisfying experience or not. Such a synthesized understanding is what one might describe as an aesthetic experience. That is, it is not assembled out of a series of isolated judgments; rather, it first reaches us in its specific totality and affects us not just intellectually, but bodily and emotionally.

Clearly the aesthetic experience has direct relevance to art, yet one might think that it is less central to design disciplines because of their demanding pragmatic and functional concerns. However, this point actually becomes *more* relevant to design *because* of its pragmatic ends; as architect Alvar Aalto says, "Nothing is as dangerous in architecture as dealing with separated problems."[22] The same can be said for design generally. The reason for this danger is twofold. First, as we discussed earlier, atomistic problem solving erases the interactions and relationships that actually constitute the problem and its possibilities. Second, the functional requirements of any design, say, for a building to stand up or a site to drain properly, can cover up the vexing aesthetic questions that every design needs to address in order to be considered well-designed. As in the restaurant example, it is the holistic impression that will first impact users, and this sense of the whole will go a long way to determining the lasting impressions, importance, and quality of any design. That is, we feel connected to, say, a French formal garden because of its beauty, which is a result of the interrelationship of things like trees, shrubbery, flowers, water, hardscape, paths, areas to sit, solar orientation, geometry, color, and views, not because of proper site grading. Now, this does not mean proper site grading is unimportant: it is critical. It just means that it is exactly this question of aesthetic impact that makes design "design" and not engineering.

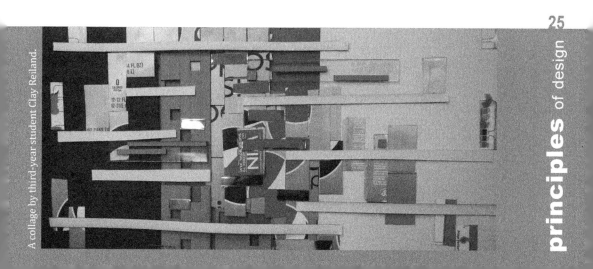

A collage by third-year student Clay Reiland.

Hampton Court Palace, London, England.

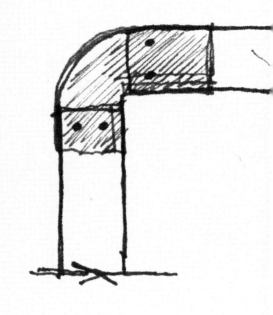

processes **of design**

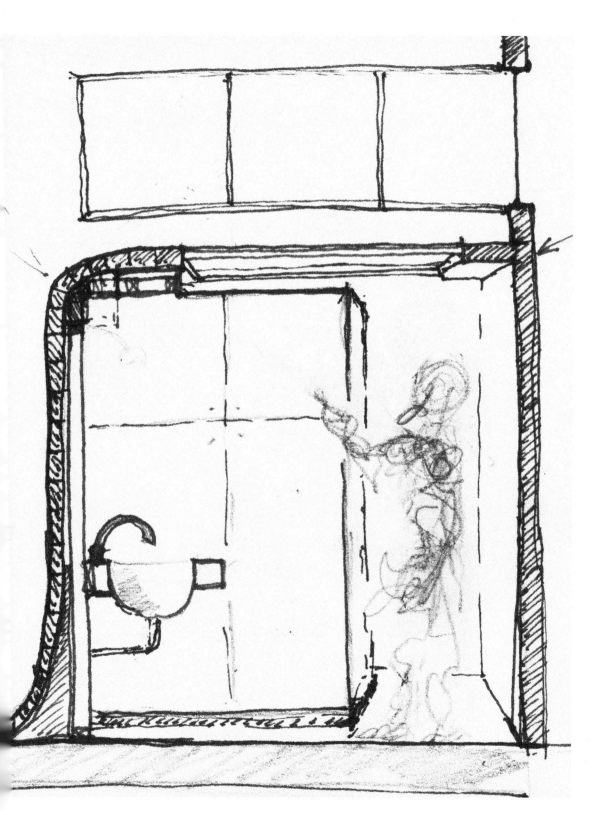

establishing habits of design
EXCELLENCE

"One who is going to listen adequately to discourse about things that are beautiful and just . . . needs to have been beautifully brought up by means of habits."[1]
Aristotle

Aristotle believed that the emergence of one's fullest self depended on establishing habits of excellence. So too, it might be argued that basic design education is also aimed at helping students develop habits of excellence—habits of *design excel-*

The tendency for our understanding of a shape that is familiar to us to retain its familiar size despite our distance from it. For example, when you see your friend 100 yards away, you don't perceive them as suddenly having gotten very small.

CONSTANCY

lence. As the phrase implies, there are both good and bad design habits, and developing habits of excellence requires learning and practicing good habits as well as unlearning bad habits.

One of the worst habits a designer can have is the kind of rationalized answer seeking that was discussed above. It is one of the worst habits not just because of the simplification it encourages in practice, but also because it is often so deeply rooted in one's psyche: that is, it can be very difficult to unlearn. Deleuze saw this habit as going back to one's early stages of development. He says:

> ... this prejudice goes back to childhood, to the classroom: it is the school teacher who "poses" the problems; the pupil's task is to discover the solutions. In this way we are kept in a kind of slavery. True freedom lies in a power to decide to constitute problems themselves.[2]

So, this particular bad habit is due, in large part, to the way our Western educational systems have trained us to test well. Testing well means that the memorization of certain prescribed facts is the key to success, risk taking is dangerous and unwise,

there are no lessons to be learned from failure, and tacit, embodied, or a-rational knowledge is as good as no knowledge at all. Typically, a focus on testing well translates into a general discomfort with any given problem that has no definitive answer; critically, as Deleuze suggests, this training leaves us with an inability to seek out and define the nature of the problems themselves. This is unfortunate because so much of the appropriateness of any solution lies in the way the problem is understood in the first place. Here, definitive answer seeking will undermine many of the most fundamental aspects of the design process—listening, experimentation, risk taking, and failing.

Design education can be a valuable experience more generally for students who have only been trained to seek answers, because its methods provide the skills for problem seeking. "Habits of excellence" is an appropriate phrase to think about design education, because the term *habit* speaks to a kind of training (and untraining) that is rooted in the entangled relationship of the whole and the particular and the importance of embodied knowledge that we discussed above. The latter is especially critical to artists and designers, because artists

We see this woman as remaining the same actual size in spite of her smaller appearance at a distance.

principles of design

and designers make things. This "making" not only produces the products of art and design, but first and foremost, is art and design's primary vehicle for thinking and developing understandings (we will discuss this more later in this section).

Finally, it is important to remember that the habits that we are seeking are not the kind that are often associated with the negative connotations of the word *habitual*—that is, obsessive, unaware, and destructive. On this point, the Mexican writer, artist, and philosopher Manuel DeLanda has observed that "while rigid habits may be enough to associate linear causes and their constant effects, they are not enough to deal with nonlinear causes that demand more adaptive, flexible skills."[3] Ensuring that the necessary flexible skills emerge begins with developing a capacity for listening.

"The Creation," Michelangelo Buonarroti.

Describes a spatial/material state where objects in proximity are understood to be in a state of continuance. Idaho is contiguous with Montana, and bricks in a brick wall are in a state of contiguity.

CONTIGUITY

LISTENING

"The position of the artist is humble, he is essentially a channel"[4]

Piet Mondrian

Film director Jim Jarmusch has spoken at length about how when he is making a movie, the story really only comes together in the editing process. That is, Jarmusch has a general idea of what the movie is about, but it is in the editing where he finds the depth of the narrative. With a similar spirit, filmmaker Terrance Malick feels that he must first build the entire world in which his film is to exist in order to find his story. For example, in his film *The New World*, Malick built the entire Jamestown settlement. Although these two methods are different in procedure, they both have at their heart the idea that the artist's job is not to simply create art, but rather, to set up the conditions for art, listen intently, and respond. As Jarmusch says, "You have to give up your ego—listen—and let the film tell *you* what it wants to be."[5]

Everything in art and design begins with listening. This is an important point to remember, because it is easy to be drawn away from the receptive aspects of design by the basic fact that designers make things: that is, they are producers. And certainly, without works of art and design, there would be no artists or designers; as Aristotle suggested, "The work of a harpist is to play the harp and the work of a serious harpist is to play the harp well."[6] So, we cannot call ourselves artists if we do not make art. However, making art begins with listening. Listening connects us to our subject matter. The following parable is an excellent dramatization of this process of connection:

> A Chinese painter was once commissioned to paint the Emperor's favorite goat. The artist asked for the goat, that he might study it. After two years the Emperor, growing impatient, asked for the return of the goat; the artist obliged. Then the Emperor asked about the painting. The artist confessed that he had not yet made one, and taking an ink brush he drew eight nonchalant strokes, creating the most perfect goat in the annals of Chinese painting.[7]

In this example, the suggestion is that intimacy of knowledge is as fundamental as an artist's skill to the making of great art, and this intimacy begins with listening well.

Contiguity: buildings along a street in the French Quarter, New Orleans, Louisiana.

principles of design

Here, the term *listening* should be understood metaphorically. This metaphoric aspect of listening indicates that we intend listening to be not just auditory, but multisensory. In this way, listening directs us to a state of attentive receptiveness, akin to what Jim Jarmusch was speaking of in the first paragraph. This peculiar notion of listening is very familiar to artists and designers and may have been most famously stated by the architect Louis Kahn. As a way of becoming more aware of the opportunities and limitations of the given material, Kahn once suggested that one should ask a brick "what it wants to be." Kahn said:

> When you want to give something presence, you have to consult nature. And there is where design comes in. And if you think of Brick, for instance, and you say to Brick, "What do you want Brick?" And Brick says to you "I like an Arch." And if you say to Brick "Look, arches are expensive, and I can use a concrete lintel over you. What do you think of that?" "Brick?" Brick says: "... I like an Arch."[8]

In other words, whether it is a raw material (Kahn's brick) or your own material (Jarmusch's film), if you listen intently, you quickly find that the things of the world have a lot to tell us. Heidegger address this point in slightly cryptic terms, saying, "If we do not want to close our eyes, we must save the phenomenon, despite, indeed even because of its 'miraculous' character. If the phenomenon itself has the first say, its clarification requires that the previous guiding

Verona Arena, Verona, Italy.

Describes a temporal or perceptual totality. In design we try to shape these totalities through our design interventions. The colors and materials used in a restaurant help give the place a sense of continuity, and the different plantings in a garden give the garden continuity. Continuity is closely related to the concept of "world" discussed in the Products of Design section of the text.

CONTINUITY

perspectives be retracted."[9] In other words, the various phenomena we experience daily have a wisdom of their own; and because of this, we should always seek to draw our understandings *from* the phenomena, *rather than imposing our ideas upon them.* This skill is critical to art and design because it helps to correct a basic fallacy of creativity—that the artist is the source of art: that is, that creativity is something inside the artist, something they bestow upon the world. Certainly this can happen, but it is probably the least effective or interesting way to think about art and design.

When art and design begin with this basic idea of listening, the work has a much greater potential to be relevant and appropriate. The reason for this is that listening well attunes us to the context and criteria that the design should be responsive to. For example, you might really like tropical huts, but if you went back home to Minnesota and built one, it would probably seem totally out of place and ultimately not function properly. The benefit (and difficulty for many) of truly listening is that it immediately immerses us in the aforementioned contingency and unpredictability of life. So the temptation is to listen, but only to a point where we find something we like, and then protect those designs, despite their perceived inappropriateness or incompleteness, against change. And this is why, using a parallel metaphor, Heidegger claimed that "a greater ill than blindness is delusion. Delusion believes that it sees, and that it sees in the only possible manner, even while this its belief robs it of sight." That is, we must be willing to hear the brick say, emphatically, "I want to be an arch," otherwise we delude ourselves into believing poor choices are actually good choices.

Even in the most literal example of listening—meeting with clients—listening does not amount to simply being able to recall what has been said; as in the parable, it means being able to discern what is significant in what has been said. In other words, it is not only important to hear and understand a client's words, but a good designer must also understand what they mean, how they are relevant to the task at hand, and ultimately what they suggest in terms of design. Here, if design were simply a one-to-one relation of a client telling the designer what they wanted, say, a granite countertop or a flagstone path, and the designer implementing that desire, then there would be, by definition, no designers.

Walker Art Center by Herzog and de Meuron, Minneapolis, Minnesota.

Path: a variety of interpretations around Kyoto, Japan.

Designers are not transcribers: they are translators. They listen and attempt to transform the words of a client into a compelling work of design. So, returning to the prior example, a designer must not only understand that there are many possibilities for what words like *countertop* and *path* (not to mention *granite* and *gravel*) might actually be, but that, like the concept of world has shown, there are a host of other forces, requirements, conditions, and relationships upon which the realization of these possibilities depend.

36

The sense that a composition does not end at the boundaries of the piece. This is a nice technique for suggesting a much larger context from a smaller work.

CONTINUANCE

the rewards of
RISK

To create anything feels risky. The reason for this feeling of risk is easy to identify: it speaks of vulnerability. In general, risky situations make us feel unsafe, which is one of the reasons our mind tells us to avoid risks—it is basic self-preservation. However, there are also reasons many seek risk as well; there is an exhilaration found in engaging activities that push our boundaries. Whether it is something literally risky, like skydiving, or something that mostly feels risky, like going to a foreign country or trying food you have never eaten before, there is a reason such frightening activities are undertaken. That is, the loss of control associated with risk reminds us how important it is to feel affected by the world around us. In fact, risk is inherent in one of the most basic human experiences—that of feeling love for someone or something other than oneself. In this way, risk could be said to be synonymous with life; and so it follows that risk is also critical to design. In fact, the importance of risk to the designer cannot be overstated.

In art and design, exposing yourself by putting something you have done up on the wall for others to comment on, and perhaps judge, can feel extremely scary. However, you must take the risk, because there is a strange irony here. When you are doing art, there will be many times when you feel you have gone too far, done something "crazy." Yet, chances are that if you respond to this feeling by toning down your work, putting up something "safe" instead, it

Matt Wilkenson, Gold Coast, Australia.

will be actually less well received than if you had pinned up what you first intended. Further, because the existence of the designer is defined by a neverending stream

"Gooyer Windmill Amsterdam." Claude Monet.

principles of design

of unique situations—a uniqueness that challenges what we know—the feeling of risk is often synonymous with appropriateness. That is, to respond to an unfamiliar situation means to make something totally new. Without a capacity for risk taking, the uniqueness of situations quickly (and falsely) transform into the commonplace and routine. So, the very act of seeing a situation in its uniqueness is a risky proposition.

Beyond the basic acceptance of the unique, design is further colored by risk because the success of any design project depends upon experimentation. Artists and designers must try things that might seem absurd, outrageous, or audacious because they just might be the perfect response to a complicated problem. If the designer is not ready to take such risks, tired, hackneyed, and inappropriate solutions quickly take over. Embracing risk brings one face to face with the necessarily non-objective nature of making. It acknowledges design as an art, in that it depends not on irrefutable facts, but rather the persuasiveness of the results.

the importance of

"While designing the Municipal Library in Viipuri, I spent a great deal of time making children's drawings. . . . In themselves these drawings had nothing to do with architecture, but from these childish drawings sprang a combination of plans and sections which, although it would be difficult to describe how, were all interwoven. And this became the basic idea of the library."[11]
Alvar Aalto

The idea of constant risk becomes more palatable when design is undertaken playfully. And not only does a state of play make risk more palatable, but a playful attitude is also an extremely effective way of working. Here, play speaks to both a disposition—being playful—as well as a manner of working that is based in problem seeking—defining the rules of the game, as it were. It is these two factors together that make play an important design tool.

Being playful, to many, seems like a trivial if not reckless way to approach serious work. Particularly in the built environment design disciplines, where health and welfare are at stake, it is easy to dismiss the notion of play outright. Yet, there is a strange generative quality that play brings to one's work. Not only does play foster creative

A context is the next larger area in which a design exists: a sculpture in a public plaza, a painting in a café, a cathedral in a medieval town, a park within a city, a bedroom within a home, a chair within a room. Not only is this nestedness a basic fact of the world we live in, as discussed throughout the book, but the interaction of context and object is a primary concern of the designer. The importance of this interaction cannot be overstated, because it is both a tremendous opportunity and a responsibility; and often it is something that designers forget.

CONTEXT

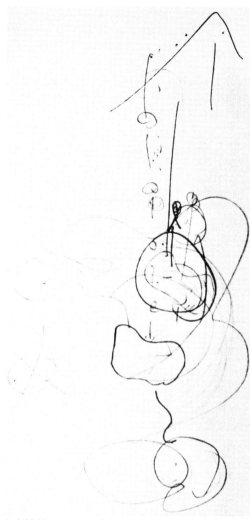

A child-like conceptual drawing.

ideas, but it also has a unique synthesizing ability. That is to say, a playful temperament can help you develop manners of working that will help you exceed your logical faculties and draw together the various concerns that cluster around any design problem.

Here, play becomes a practice that allows a designer to transform the threats of risk into opportunities. This is due, in part, to the fact that feelings of risk are almost always present because one is anticipating a result. Play does not care for ends: it takes joy in playing. In other words, play allows one to become invested in the work at hand without worrying over consequences and results. I emphasize this last point because often an over-focus on conclusions distracts necessary attention away from ideation and development, causing us to second-guess ideas. In short, a playful and focused engagement helps us avoid premature ends as well as helping us to escape that feeling of being "stuck." The latter often occurs simply because one is thinking rather than working, or better—playing.

Rules are a critical part of play, because without limits the structure of any game

principles of design

The context for the city of Banff, Alberta.

For example, in architecture, students will frequently work on their buildings as if they are objects with generic space inside and generic space surrounding. However, the built environment is made up of specific interrelated places that are framed by specific contexts of differing scales. Thought of in this way, a building becomes a context for a number of different activities, and the walls that shape "rooms" of the city.

Match between BVB Dortmund and VfB Stuttgart.

tion, make a productive frame, so that something might be played with. In a literal sense, the game of soccer can occur if one has a pitch, 11 players on each side, 45-minute halves, a soccer ball, goals, and the necessary rules to define fair play and game procedures. However, even when using the specific equipment and following the rules of the game, there is still a reasonable amount of space for interpretation (play). Musical improvisation works in a similar fashion—needing some form of musical structure for the musical-play of improvisation to happen.

Providing similar types of definition and limits is important to facilitate design. Certainly the design problems you will be given begin to lay out some limits and possibilities for your design; however, often the basic description of the problem is not enough to create a productive space that inspires and questions. You need to give it an identity, something that pushes back. That is, play space is not simply a place to play, but a place that encourages play. As in the example of a soccer game, one needs both the physical (pitch and equipment)

disintegrates. Imagine for a moment that someone left you in an empty room and said, "Play." Well, without any elements suggesting how to play, it would probably be an uninspiring game. Instead of desiring to be totally free, we always seek specificity in our play. For example, children will often assign very particular traits, names, and functions to their dolls, race cars, fire trucks, and such. These "rules" help to make the game more real.

Spielraum is a German word that literally means "play-room," and it speaks of the need to circumscribe an area of explora-

A datum is a point of reference. It can be a point, line, surface, or proposition, and is used as a construct to help one organize or make decisions. For example, in the case of a line, it is similar to an axis. However, instead of being a line connecting two distinct points, it is a line that divides (or organizes) two halves. In other words, it is a normalizing condition that collects a series of elements along its length. If the linear datum is a significant demarcation between two different conditions, it becomes a threshold.

DATUM

Improvisation: Maceo Parker.

the dynamics of
DESIGNING

"Always design a thing by considering it in its next larger context—a chair in a room, a room in a house, a house in an environment, an environment in a city plan."[12]
Eliel Saarinen

Street art under a freeway, Boise, Idaho.

and the mental (rules, limits, provocations) to energize the activity.

Now, as a playful, risk-taking person who knows how to listen, you are ready to engage the fullness of the design process.

A wall being used as an organizing datum, Eugene, Oregon.

In order for designers to successfully deal with the dynamic relationships of our world, they must be able to visualize both complexity and a process of working with complexity. The partnership of French theorists Gilles Deleuze and Felix Guattari produced a magnificent visualization of the dynamic unity of the world with their concept of the "rhizome."

The rhizome describes the way that life is comprised of and largely shaped by unpredictable forces, flows, interactions, collisions, and transformations. That is, life is not something fundamentally stable that gets disrupted from time to time: rather, life is something dynamic and unstable that congeals, coagulates, and coalesces to form situations, events, institutions, and places, as well as the objects of art and design. They describe the rhizome:

> A rhizome as subterranean stem is absolutely different from roots and radicles. Bulbs and tubers are rhizomes . . . Even some animals are, in their pack form. Rats are rhizomes . . . When rats swarm over each other. The rhizome includes the best and the worst: potato and couchgrass, or the weed. . . . any point of a rhizome can be connected to anything other, and must be. This is very different from the tree or root, which plots a point, fixes an order.[13]

Rhizome: swarming honeybees.

There are two kinds of depth we talk about in a design: literal and existential. Here we will talk about literal depth. Literal depth in environmental design is exactly what it sounds like—a palpable feeling of space; however, when we are concerned with literal depth, we are typically concerned with the illusion of depth in representation. This kind of depth is generally communicated via overlapping parts and similar elements that diminish in scale (things that are further away from us appear smaller), or via perspective. Linear perspective is primarily a technique used in the West, and comparing a Western perspective to a Japanese print provides a good example of two different notions about achieving depth in representation.

DEPTH

With this concept, Deleuze and Guattari are highlighting the difference between a more open, dynamic way of thinking that engages the unpredictabilities of life and our reductive thinking, which tends to visualize and produce "arborescent" systems. In contrast to more rhizomatic systems, arborescent thinking yields systems with hierarchical coherence emanating from a central "trunk," and suggests growth toward a specific end [DIAGRAM]. For example, our school systems are structured this way—a student moves in a hierarchical straight line from grade to grade—as are most large business organizations, which are typically composed of the hierarchy of upper management, middle management, and workers.

Alternately, rhizomatic thinking engages and activates the nonlinear compound interactions that shape our lives. It is something we are capable of but often unaware of, because of our tendency to seek coherence and order. For example, you interacted with a variety of forces, flows, collisions, and transformations in order to be in the place where you are sitting right now. If you were to try to explain this process with any degree of precision, most likely, you would feel overwhelmed, because you would quickly encounter an improbable collection of different factors, which in retrospect make some sense, but are simply difficult to diagram or articulate clearly because of their asymmetrical effects. However, you were clearly able to navigate this complexity. This often overlooked ability we have to navigate complexity reminds us that there is a difference between the arbitrary and the ambiguous; a rhizomatic system is the former. *Arbitrary* implies that no relationships exist whatsoever and everything just happens on a whim, whereas *ambiguous*

PHD

MASTERS DEGREE

BACHELORS DEGREE

HIGH SCHOOL DIPLOMA

GRAMMAR SCHOOL

A typical arborescent organizational chart.

"Place de l'Europe on a Rainy Day,"
Gustave Caillebotte (top). "Yoshida,"
Ando Hiroshige (bottom).

Other techniques for producing depth include: inverse perspective (seen often in medieval drawings), where lines *diverge* toward the viewer; amplified perspective, where artists use the techniques of perspective drawing in extreme ways to destabilize, heighten, and distort the rigidity of the normal mode of perspective representation; and simultaneous perspective, where a representation includes multiple viewpoints, either from different viewers at the same time or by introducing the element of time into the composition as Cubism did.

principles of design

A rhizomatic system: bats seeking food at night.

means that the relationships are hard to discern or make explicit, but they are there nonetheless. In short, rhizomatic thinking is our means of engaging and creating ambiguous systems.

The Internet is an excellent example of this kind of ambiguous system. Like the other rhizomatic forms and processes described above, the Internet is dynamic and decentralized, resists predictability, and functions despite its seeming lack of order. In the Internet, "any point [is] . . . connected to anything other." Further, the way the Internet works emphasizes the need for expanding our definitions of thinking. This is because the Internet has completely refocused the nature of knowledge, calling into question the memorization and retrieval model of intelligence. In other words, the Internet has already "memorized" a seemingly inexhaustible pool of data for us, so knowing facts personally becomes less important than our ability to (a) know what we are looking for and (b) have the skills to find it. Further, on the Internet, data is only as good as its presentation and the robustness of your search engine. That is, all the information is there waiting for us, so knowledge becomes not about who knows the most stuff, but rather who can ask the

A diagram is a drawing or object that attempts to elementalize some complex phenomenon in order to make it more understandable and usable. For instance, diagrams are often included with the instructions we receive with a new product in order to make its assembly and/or use more apparent.

Typically, diagrams are a way of making a complicated verbal or written description more easily understood. For designers, this point has two significances. First, a diagram is in itself a design problem; that is, doing a good diagram often takes making and remaking the diagram many

DIAGRAM

ARBORESCENT THINKING

linear steps to find the goal

linear steps building gradually to the goal

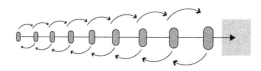

iterative steps building gradually to the goal

spiraling inward towards goal

RHIZOMATIC THINKING

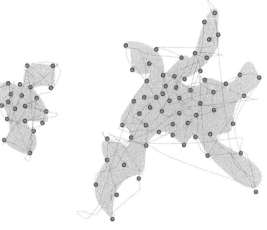

a series of interconnected moves continually
interact and inform growing into a networked
understanding that is the goal

An organizational diagram for a house remodel.

times, because it is difficult to make something that says so much with such visual economy—in fact, it is the correct use of visual economy that allows a diagram to speak well. Second, doing diagrams will help you, as a designer, take ownership of your work intellectually and verbally, because diagrams demand that you articulate what your work is about, what matters to the way it functions, and why we should care about it in the first place.

Diagrams are extremely powerful if you take them seriously and practice making them; and they go hand-in-hand with analyzing, synthesizing, and communicating data.

principles of design

best questions, and who is most adept at defining problems and inquiring into their answers. The Internet, as a rhizomatic system, shows us how much of our world is organized organically—it possesses both the dynamics of chaos and the connections of an ordered system. Understanding the real dynamics of the design process is greatly aided by the rhizome.

Traditionally, design process has been visualized arborescently. In this visualization, design is seen to rely upon the finding of a brilliant initial idea—planting the seed, as it were—and then developing it into a fully formed design. Unfortunately, this model has a lot of problems. First, work will frequently stagnate as one fishes around for the *best* idea before moving forward. Next, because this model is linear, when things do not go as planned, it appears as if you have "failed" and therefore must "start over." In other words, if the project appears to hit a dead end, the tree in effect dies and therefore a new seed must be planted. Such frustrating experiences are embedded in the linearity, monolithicness, and inflexibility of the tree. Here, the arborescent model says that everything in the development of a design must be heaped upon prior correct decisions. Such a visualization of design is both unproductive and stressful.

If, instead, we think of design as a rhizomatic system, we enact a process that mirrors the actualities that we will be working with. Perhaps most critically, the rhizome shows us that project development is not constrained to a linear path. That is, the rhizome reinforces the idea that connections and breakthroughs often happen in unpredictable ways, and that these occurrences are, in fact, neither random nor arbitrary. Further, the decentered nature of the rhizome mitigates the controlling desires of the thinking-I, because when the design process is viewed as being rhizomatic, designers no longer need to see themselves as creators or conductors, as sovereign agents standing outside a design regulating the process. Instead, designers become participants, or perhaps better, a force. Heidegger drives this point home, saying:

> It is precisely in great art—and only such art is under consideration here—that the artist remains inconsequential as compared with the work, almost like a passageway that destroys itself in the creative process for the work to emerge.[14]

In other words, the control that the "thinking-I" is constantly trying to assert is not only unnecessary, but is actually something

Duration addresses the fact that virtually everything we do is done over a span of time. Some durations are more certain—a movie, a flight from New York to Boston—whereas others can be indeterminate, like a baseball game or a conversation with a friend.

Despite the fact that duration is basic to how we live in this world, we often have difficulty imagining, visualizing, and working with time. This is a critical point for designers, because it raises the necessity of not only imagining a design as a special moment, but also how it is to persist and be experienced over a course of time.

DURATION

that undermines the process of making art and design, because it undervalues the other factors and forces such as material, culture, climate, history, and so on that should be at least as influential as the artist alone.

However, one cannot simply visualize the design process as being rhizomatic and proceed to correct the deficiencies of the thinking-I; one must also develop the kind of thinking that will make this visualization effectual.

INTUITIVE THINKING

"Intellect wishes to arrange—intuition wishes to accept."[15]
Georgia O'Keeffe

"Okabe," Ando Hiroshige.

The effects of time, Palouse, Washington.

How long should a viewer be asked to look at a work of art? How drawn out should the walk between buildings on a campus be? How will a landscape mature as it grows up over a number of years?

The questions of duration are essential to design, but are often hard for the designer to discern and design for.

principles of design

Becoming comfortable with the ambiguity of the design process can release you from the unproductive practices of "figuring it out in your head" or trying to devise rules for making good design. However, in order to overcome such rationalizations one must create. That is to say, it is necessary not to simply try to *think* differently, but to think by leaping into the work. A leap here means no matter how much preparation, analysis, or research you do, there will always be a moment when you must start designing. Intuition occurs when one becomes immersed in their project.

A helpful way to facilitate such immersion is by being attentive to matters close at hand, or as Heidegger says, "Underway, then—we must give particularly close attention to that stretch of way on which we are putting our feet."[16] This is a point that seems somewhat paradoxical when a design needs to be concerned with achieving particular ends. And yet Heidegger's intent is to remind us that there is a certain loss of perspective that is required for real participation. He explains this idea, saying, "A specific kind of forgetting is essential for . . . letting something be involved. The Self must forget itself if . . . it is to be able 'actually' to go to work and manipulate something."[17]

Deleuze and Guattari apply this idea to art, saying:

> The law of the painting is that it is to be done at close range, even if it is to be viewed from relatively far away. One can back away from a thing, but it is the bad painter who backs away from the painting he or she is working on . . . Cézanne spoke of the need to *no longer be able to see* the wheat field, to be too close to it, to lose oneself without landmarks in smooth space.[18]

Landscape by Paul Cézanne.

In other words, too much distance can bring too much reflection, which ultimately begets second-guessing and hence timidity. In this way, the ability to not think about

The state of being in flux, or the suggestion of movement.

DYNAMIC

yourself, your past, the design brief, or the design product you are working on is an important skill and a required aspect of effective design thinking. Here, we are not to imagine that we throw all these concerns out entirely; rather, design thinking requires that the information you have "forgotten" be retained in a rather remarkable way. Heidegger explains this phenomenon as follows:

> Thinking clears its own way only by its own questioning advance. But this clearing of the way is curious. The way that is cleared does not remain behind, but is built into the next step, and is projected forward from it.[19]

That is, each move you make reveals insights that lead to other insights, and all these insights ultimately coalesce around the things you make. In this manner, thinking opens a path for itself and all of your thoughts, concerns, and ideas. What all this means is that is that it is actually more productive for you to become deeply involved in your work, forgetting your concerns, because there is an intelligence at work here; and just because you are forgetting some things does not mean that you will actually forget them. For example, sometimes students will want to make a "simple" design. Simple is difficult because there is such a fine line between simple and boring. So, in a case like this, it is usually better to start off by being more expressive and experimental and forget about simple, because in the end you will have something worth simplifying. In this way, you can bring along a sensibility that was not helpful as a beginning, and allow it to find its place in the end.

Part of the reason we are having to learn about this kind of thinking is that Western cultures have generally been uncomfortable with intuition. However, there are other cultures that have long been connected to the intuitive mind. Diasetsu Suzuki describes why many Eastern cultures value intuition:

> There is truth in saying that the Oriental mind is intuitive while the Western mind is logical and discursive. An intuitive mind has its weaknesses, it is true, but its strongest point is demonstrated when it deals with things most fundamental in life, that is, things related to religion, art, and metaphysics.[20]

Fish carving, Kyoto, Japan.

So, in the East, intuition is seen as our primary access to spirituality and art; and it is because of this, and our reliance upon the logical, that intuition is frequently categorized as a mystical kind of facility in the West. This characterization is both good and bad. It is good because it highlights the importance of the ephemeral aspects of any pursuit that can be properly regarded as an art and the need to employ parallel processes to engage them. That is, one cannot simply will art into being through purely rational means.

The negative impact of intuition being thought of as something mystical is that, like art itself, such a framing can make intuition subject to dismissal on the grounds

"Hakone," Ando Hiroshige.

What is the point of highest contrast in that painting? Where does the axis terminate? What place is created by the use of certain geometry?

When a designer places emphasis on a certain part of a work, it can not only create a focus, but set up a sense of tension and/or harmony in the work. It can allow viewers and users to orient themselves and to have a place of departure and return.

EMPHASIS

that it is not real, no better than opinion, and merely a self-serving justification of something that should be placed under more rigorous scrutiny. In short, framing intuition as mystical denies the basic underpinnings and connections to the world that make it a valid means of engagement. Intuition is not magical: it functions when one is prepared. Intuition is deeply tied to our habits, which is why we aspire to make these habits "excellent."

Compared to the type of knowledge that is presented to us by the thinking-I—knowledge that is held out in front of our mind's eye like a carrot—intuition seems mystical because its knowledge does not manifest with definite origins and implications. This difference often leads intuitive knowledge to be treated as not having the same worth as rational knowledge (or even being knowledge at all). The difference between these two types of knowledge is something like the difference between the information contained in a map (thinking-I) versus the knowledge of one who has lived in a certain place for a long time (intuition). In the latter case, one simply knows how to get around. So, in contrast to the knowledge of the thinking-I, intuitive knowledge manifests as we do things, and because of this, it

is often hard to grasp or talk about. For example, try to explain to someone how to ride a bike. However, like the rhizome, just because something is complicated and hard to define does not make it "mystical." Intuition is something that can be learned, practiced, and improved.

Intuitive knowledge is fostered through continual engagement with an activity and manifests as an ability to make certain judgments or come to certain realizations. The results of intuitive knowledge may appear arbitrary, but when examined retrospectively they often demonstrate a great degree of exactness, insight, and substance. For designers, intuitive knowledge is indispensable. For example, a trained landscape architect needs to have a knowledge of, say, the species of all the trees on a given site, but without also being able to see patterns, subtle shifts in topography, and possibilities for design therein, the former information is useless. Sometimes, intuition brings us an "aha" sort of insight in these situations, but more often than not it is through working on the project—sketching, walking the site, making maps, diagramming ideas, and drawing visions—that one enters into intuitive understanding.

Emphasis: DeYoung Museum, San Francisco, California.

Multiple points of emphasis can be a way of creating continuity as well as tension.

principles of design

Sketching as a means of "becoming" place, Florence, Italy.

Deleuze and Guattari used a term, *becoming*, which is helpful in connecting with the habitual aspect of the intuitive. In this concept they suggest, "We are not *in* the world, we *become with* the world; we become by contemplating it . . . Van Gogh's sunflowers are becomings, like Dürer's thistles or Bonnard's mimosas."[21] So, becoming speaks less to the "aha" of intuitive insight, and more to the process of developing embodied knowledge itself. Deleuze and Guattari go on to say becoming is "an extreme contiguity within a coupling of two sensations without resemblance."[22] What they mean here is that Van Gogh does not come to resemble a sunflower while studying and painting it, nor do the sunflowers he paints come to have a physical resemblance to Van Gogh; rather, the painting is a synthesis of these two entities, both Van Gogh and sunflower. As he goes through the process of painting the sunflower, the intensity of focus has, in a way, allowed Van Gogh to become a sunflower: the sunflower is now part of him as an embodied understanding. Again, becoming is not mystical, and we all will experience this kind of synthesis when we spend, say, an hour drawing a tree. In fact, you will probably be surprised to find that drawing with such focus will leave a deep, unreasoned, and indelible understanding of the tree (or whatever else you might choose to draw). In this way, "becoming" speaks to the link between the artist and their world that is created through their work. Here, artist, world, and work, in essence, become the same thing, with the artist coming to know her project as she would know herself.

The word *existential* pertains to existence. It is often associated with the philosophical movement known as existentialism. In general, this term has to do with understanding and knowing things by way of experience, and how the manner in which we live tends to define us. Existentialism is interested in the world as we find it and not our definitions of it.

EXISTENTIAL

"Sunflowers," Vincent Van Gogh.

principles of design

The intuitive is the designer's means of discerning that sense of wholeness in a situation and connecting its potentialities to one's vast knowledge and skills; it critically links to the Greek notion of art—*techne*.

art as
TECHNE

Beer making in the Unyamwezi region, Tanzania.

"Only when man speaks does he think."[23]
Martin Heidegger

Design thinking, too, only really speaks through the things it makes. For the Greeks the interconnection between thinking and making was captured by the term *techne*. Heidegger saw great power in this concept and was also very worried about the fact that it had increasingly come to refer less to art and more to our utilization of advanced technology to make our lives easier. In much of his writing, he sought to re-enliven some of the lost insights of the Greek usage of the term.

Originally, the notion of art suggested in *techne* not only pointed to technical mastery of certain tools, but also was inseparable from a kind of sensitive attention that went along with the use of these tools. So in a sense, *techne* is like an amalgam of listening and intuition extended into the tools of a craft. And because of this, *techne* spoke not just of the fine arts but also more generally of crafts and specialized practices. This view of art could apply to cabinetmaking, navigation, or politics just as well as to painting or sculpture.

Such a general understanding of "art" was embraced because it was seen that a unique combination of disciplinary knowledge, manual dexterity, and acuity of vision was required for the success of these kinds of pursuits. That is, one must exhibit both physical skills and mental sharpness for a practice to be called art. *Techne* is a special type of knowledge, in part, because it is a

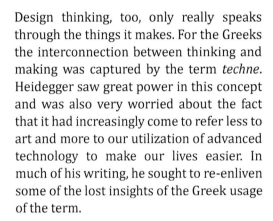

This is a term pair that signifies a relationship of significance between an object and the space surrounding it. Often the term *figure/ground* is used when speaking of urban maps. Here, the built forms are the figures and the negative space is the space of the city. The idea here is that when there is a good balance between figure and ground, there is strength in the composition, because both the objects and the space around them are seen to have a presence and a clarity.

FIGURE/GROUND

of thinking we have been discussing above is the fact that its wisdom is uniquely responsive to the dynamics of nature (*physis*). Such an understanding of creation helps to emphasize the link between design and the world around us: that is, design as something that addresses, and even emanates from, problems and possibilities within the world (as opposed to just making cool stuff).

knowledge made manifest though the making (*poiesis*) of things. In this way, *techne* is different than say, *episteme*, which is a knowledge that is possessed—I simply know (or not) what a giraffe is, that 2+2=4, that a water molecule is made of one oxygen atom and two hydrogen atoms, et cetera. Further connecting *techne* to the types

For the Greeks the world was dynamic, active, growing, made up of an agglomeration of interconnected entities and events. Energizing this world was the "self-blossoming emergence" of *physis*.[24] For the Greeks, this meant they were constantly experiencing feelings of surprise and wonder and of being enmeshed in a dynamic and vital

principles of design

environment. In short, the term *physis* suggests a world where potency and mystery are truly felt in every situation: seeds transforming into trees and plants, flowers blooming, animals being born, living, and dying, the sun rising and setting, storms moving in and passing on, seasons changing, and so on. In *physis* we have an understanding of nature and the processes of life where one still is captivated by a sunny day, a powerful storm, a chance encounter with a wild animal, or the birds singing on an early spring morning.

Techne is connected to *physis,* but differs because it is concerned with objects of human use. Unlike nature, objects of human use do not come about through "self-blossoming emergence." That is, they need our assistance, because they cannot arise of their own accord. However, objects of human use are connected to nature by way of *techne*. Here, *techne* referred to the specifically human ability to "reveal that which does not bring itself forth."[25] What this means is that we have a capacity to see the potential within the world around us and draw it out through our making of things. Here, an "artist" is able to recognize certain traits or circumstances that offer the things of the world alternate potentials from their

natural ends. In short, *physis* deals with natural ends and *techne* speaks to those ends that can only come about with human intervention. However, the critical point to understand here, and why this is an important idea for designers, is that the connection between *physis* and *techne* suggests that the stuff of nature has possibilities *already built into it*, and that these are possibilities that can *almost* make themselves. As artists we are merely helping the world show its latent potential.

Here, the artist is not creating from a nature that is seen as a collection of raw materials or resources; rather, the artist is, like Jarmusch and Kahn suggested, freeing something to be *what it already wants to be*. So for example, it is possible to "free" a dugout canoe from a tree. This is a particular capacity of wood (a dugout canoe cannot be made from dirt, animal skins, or granite), and only particular types of trees in particular locations with particular dimensions allow for this type of "creation." *Techne* is the realization of particular possibilities inherent to particular things in particular contexts that cannot come to be through the basic processes of nature (*physis*).

Final projects are rarely final. In fact, one learns quite quickly that it is the *act of trying to make something final* that is critical to the production of quality design. The act of trying to make something final brings new levels of discovery and refinement.

For better or worse, actually finishing a design requires "finishing" it about a hundred times. In other words, the commitment and follow-through that come with trying to finish something reveal and clarify things about your work that are not possible when you are merely thinking, testing, or dabbling; and although these other processes are

FINISHING

Just to be clear, let us think about this in another way. Given the right environment, an acorn naturally grows into an oak tree: it frees itself. An oak tree, however, does not become a table through its own accord. Instead, it requires someone to see its potential to become this particular object of use and to possess the specific skills to make this vision happen. A skilled artist not only knows to use oak instead of some other less suited species, but also knows which parts of the tree will be better for different

The results of *techne*: a cobbled stone street in Gruyere, France.

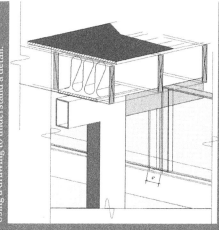

Using a drawing to understand a detail.

important, they do not substitute for the kind of information that "finishing" brings. In short, finishing seeks to prove and explain certain details, and in so doing, it also shows those details that need more attention, those that are not consistent, those that have been neglected, and those that begin to define your design.

purposes and how to read the grain of the wood in ways that will aid the craft of the object, planning for the dynamic expansion and shrinkage that go along with using this specific type of wood in this particular climate and application. So, in this way, *techne* describes human beings participating in and affecting a dynamic self-transforming environment. Here, to be an artist or designer means to recognize and engage the ways in which one's environment is always already filled with significance and possibilities.

"Flowers," Odilon Redon.

However, this practice need not be limited to nature. As was stated at the beginning of this section, such a notion of "freeing" can be thought of as more generally applicable to the practices of art and design. For example, Zen Master Shunryu Suzuki suggested, "A wonderful painting is the result of a feeling in your fingers . . . if you have the feeling of the thickness of the ink in your brush, the painting is already there before you paint."[26] This view of life is possible for us, but often is obstructed by all of the distractions that go along with modern life. With this in mind, we come to one of the primary responsibilities of the artist—trying to recover such a *thick* experience of the world. When this occurs, art reconnects with *techne*.

However, to be effective, artists must not only develop sensitivity: they must also develop a commitment to their work.

A design is subject to both external and internal forces. External forces are things like client, site, a particular culture, or climate; internal forces have to do with questions related to continuity, composition, and search for integrity in a design.

FORCES

design
FAITH

". . . a paradoxical and humble courage is required to grasp the whole of the temporal by virtue of the absurd, and this courage is faith."[27]
Søren Kierkegaard

Danish philosopher Søren Kierkegaard had an idea about the ways we might best conduct ourselves in our lives. He came up with a concept, "the knight of faith," that was derived from medieval chivalric love to indicate one who has the faith to commit oneself wholly to a situation that is seemingly "absurd": that is, caring unreservedly for another human being, *knowing* that this situation is contingent, vulnerable, and out of one's ultimate control.[28] Further, there is a paradox in this "absurd" condition where it is *the act of commitment* (not what one is committing to) that forms the genuineness

Guthrie Theater by Jean Nouvel. Minneapolis, Minnesota.

"Tornado Bahamas," Winslow Homer.

59

principles of design

and depth of the commitment. In other words, one does not become a knight of faith by waiting, weighing, and measuring, seeking an ideal so irresistible that one cannot do anything but commit to it. Instead, making a commitment in spite of uncertainty to a specific, temporal, and vulnerable situation is the initiation of meaning. In short, Kierkegaard's basic message is that without a commitment made through faith (i.e., one that is not reasoned, calculated, or measured), one remains in a passionless existence. Without a commitment, one is without a world.

This concept is relevant to designers because activating the creative process demands an analogous act of commitment. And, similar to the paradox that the knight of faith encounters, designers will often think that achieving a design that is whole and refined requires that you first know what the whole is; but this reasoning and focus on the universal is exactly what Kierkegaard is reacting against. The commitment begets the whole, not the other way around. So, when we believe an early idea or experiment to be the design solution, we deny the developmental process that is central to the practice of design. That is,

you can easily trap yourself with a superficial design product by taking your first idea not as a beginning (which implies much still needs to be worked out), but as the design itself. Such a conception of one's work has the unwanted effect of causing the investigative side of the design process—where more and more factors are encountered, considered, and incorporated—to get shut down. This point is important because it highlights the difference between the process and the products of design.

In the design process, anything goes. This optimistic attitude will further the development of your design, because it recognizes that you are in no way obligated to keep, make, or even show the things you produce along the way. You only owe your client a brilliant product. However, the probability of such a result is increased through the rigor of your process. Process and product are intimately connected, but often not the same. In most design projects, for example, designers often forget the drawings are not the actual design. Rather, a drawing is, as Alberto Perez-Gomez calls it, "a mediating artifact."[29] This point highlights two things: (a) that there is a difference in kind between a drawing and its ultimate end,

A three-dimensional closed object.

FORM

which indicates that the criteria by which they are evaluated are, in fact, different; and (b) that if the artifacts of the design process are thought of as mediating elements, then we are granted more freedom to explore even the most seemingly outrageous possible solutions—and this depends upon the "play" of process. Ulti-mately, because the artifacts of the design process are different in kind from the final products, *we owe it to the life of the final product* to take advantage of the amazing opportunities afforded by the design process as an incubational period to play, take risks, experiment, and investigate the unknown. When this does not occur, we end

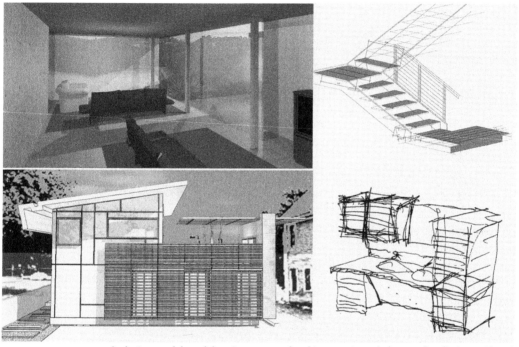

In design, models and drawings are not the objects we intend: they are "mediating artifacts."

Apartments, Eugene, Oregon.

principles of design

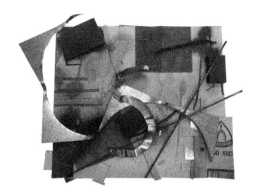

Design experiments: studies for a firehouse, third-year students Megan Wigton and Matt Garner.

you somewhere than to wait, measure, and try to ensure the right choice is being made. Cultivating even those ideas that are seemingly weird does what continuous reflection, calculation, and waiting cannot—*it opens up the world of the project*. Here, design can actually progress, because such an opening-up shows the designer the path to success (and failure). You begin to be able to see what matters and what does not, and you begin to care.

Ultimately, finding one's passion for *precisely* those slightly odd or incomplete things acknowledges and embraces the fact that any creation does not arrive fully formed; most creative works start as a strange, even disconcerting, microscopic potentiality. Such recognition of the necessary unfamiliarity of pure potential and an ongoing commitment to said uncertainty through design can evolve to become great work. In this way, the "knight of faith" is a fitting model for the successful designer. As designers, we are always having to exist in a space of faith, loving those beautiful experiments we create, yet knowing they might be taken away by other more relevant concerns and that no matter how stuck we might feel, a project will always come together.

up with malformed designs. In this way, the design process and the designer's commitment to its objects are the engines that make design happen and make design successful.

We might call this practice "design faith," as it suggests that often it is simply more important to *invest in something* and let it take

The Cartesian grid is probably the most familiar grid; it consists of intersecting lines in three dimensions and a corresponding x,y,z coordinate system. For designers, the grid is a basic organizational system that can help bring order, precision, and readability to their work. Grids are used in typography and web design, as well as graphic design more generally, but are also employed in the environmental design disciplines and art. In art, Piet Mondrian authored some of the most iconic grid-based works.

GRID

critical thinking =
PRECISION

When I give a dictionary definition of a table—a horizontal flat surface supported by three or four legs, which can be used for eating off, reading a book on, and so forth—I may feel that I have got, as it were, to the essence of the table . . . In this example, however, I am not perceiving but rather defining. By contrast, when I perceive a table, I do not withdraw my interest from the particular way it has of performing its function as a table . . . What interests me is the unique movement from the feet to the table top which resists gravity; this is what makes each table different from the next. No detail is insignificant: the grain, the shape of the feet, the color and age of the wood, as well as the scratches or graffiti, which show that age. The meaning, "table" will only interest me insofar as it arises out of all the "details," which embody its present mode of being.[30]

Maurice Merleau-Ponty

Now that we have re-established the importance of our a-rational abilities, it is time to describe the effective use of our rational abilities. We will do this through the concept of critical thinking. Critical thinking is the ability to filter irrelevancies, to discern possibilities, and to make judgments. The ability to think critically is rooted in both imagination and doubt. That is, thinking critically demands that one be able to generate options and opportunities while simultaneously being able to question one's own intentions and beliefs, as well as the results of one's experiments. Without an effective practice of critical thinking, a designer's work will lack

It is not the definition (table) that is important but rather the specific instance of that definition and the particulars that go with it.

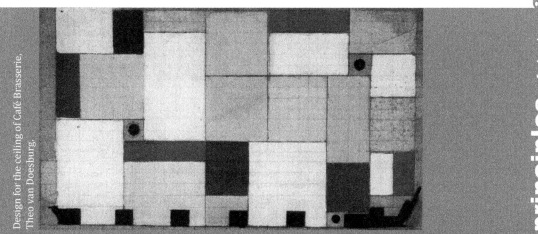

Design for the ceiling of Café Brasserie, Theo van Doesburg.

principles of design

precision in the way it addresses a given problem. That is to say, what frequently occurs when one is not thinking critically is that proposed design intervention will not be re-measured against the criteria one was designing for in the first place. Thus it will be lacking in intensity, appropriateness, and finish. For example, in a project where students were asked to create a design that somehow amplified or altered a viewer's perception of a real place, many students started off with astute observations about the place, and proceeded to posit a reasonable response to said observation; but then, a majority took this initial positing to be the end result (just what we talked about not doing above!). With this oversight, these students overlooked flaws or missed opportunities in the proposed solution. When one does not revisit the problem with the rigor of critical thinking, designs lack precision. However, this is a very special notion of precision. Vittorio Gregotti describes this kind of precision:

Precision means the ability to describe nuances with exactitude; an ability to see through things with subtlety, to know and weigh the value of a detail, to understand the significance of absences, of pauses, of emptiness, of variation, and of the relationship between architectural objects as well as their individual forms. Precision means that every piece of the project, however small, must be entirely legible, revealing not only its own independence, but the necessity behind both its existence and its connections with other elements, as well as the reasons why each of those elements was selected.

The reasons for these choices must, in turn, be intelligible when they are offered as a deliberate turn away from consistency in a project, so that each solution shows itself to be the only point of balance within the labyrinth of possible solutions.[31]

Following this quote, then, it seems that the type of precision we are here concerned with is sensitivity to the specifics of a given situation and how accurately one's design addresses these specifics. So, for instance, if we return to the previous example, we see one student who observed an area where residents tended to gather within one of the student housing complexes. In identifying this gathering point,

Key frame is a term that is typically associated with filmmaking and animation. It refers to the set points between particular movements. For example, in animation it might be that Mickey Mouse starts holding a baseball and ends in a frame where he has just released the ball from his hand. From these key frames, the animator can begin to reckon about the moments in between.

Key frames can also be thought of metaphorically in the built environment disciplines as the key moments of experience as one moves through a design. This not

KEY FRAME

A key moment in a competition proposal for Octavia Boulevard, San Francisco, California.

only helps to draw a temporal line through the experience, but also helps designers think about key moments that should be memorable.

principles of design

the student also noticed that the bench that helped to designate this gathering place was not particularly supportive of the groups that gathered there.

He imagined that there could be an intervention that both underscored the location and provided better accommodation to a variety of potential uses, particularly supporting conversation. In response to this problem, he proposed erecting a tepee, because to him it represented a form that would both mark the site and encourage conversation. This was an excellent start. Unfortunately, the student designer quickly became wedded to the tepee, despite the culturally loaded nature of its iconic presence, as well as the fact that building a tepee would certainly exceed the $200 budget that had been given to the students. Not until the oddity and/or potential dismissal of the tepee by other students (i.e., taking its presence to be indicative of a Native American Club project or the like) got recognized as a problem could it be reinvestigated by way of the budget limitation. Because of this reassessment of both the problem itself and the student's design intentions, the student put himself in a position to produce something that was te-

pee-inspired, but consequently dug deeper into the specific demands of the design problem. In short, it was a project that moved toward a more compelling solution, exactly because the designer sought greater precision.

In this example, there is a critical lesson about the importance of making things in order to help our observations and ideas more complete and accurate. As Manuel DeLanda describes:

> Analysis must go beyond logic and involve *causal interventions in reality* such as lesions made to an organ within an organism, or the poisoning of enzymes within a cell, followed by observations of the effect on the whole's behaviour.[32]

In other words, the act of proposing an actual solution (tepee) provides far more feedback and information to the designer than merely muddling about with vague notions of, say, an enhanced gathering place. Here, the physical artifacts of design can be clearly understood as powerful manifestations of one's thinking and provide stimulation for ideas (mental or written) that simply cannot be found by just

Light, either actual or perceptual, can be a powerful activator for a design. The painters of the Italian Renaissance made great use of contrast to activate their scenes; medieval builders, using stained glass, made God material in the light of the great cathedrals; interior designers have become masters of lighting effects that change the atmosphere of a place; and landscape designers have sometimes strategically removed light to create areas of shade and repose where one might sit and spend the afternoon in a park or garden.

LIGHT

mentally searching for them. However, the effectiveness of making things in order to determine what one should ultimately make depends, again, upon understanding that every design move is provisional. So, like we discussed above, when we take our first idea to be the final solution, we short-circuit the generative aspects of making and undermine the incremental growth that fosters the precision we are aiming for. In this process, making our first solutions concrete is important, again with the idea that these are provisional, because in transferring an idea into material and form we are given something we can test, evaluate—in short, think about *critically*. The rationale here is that we will necessarily produce something perhaps interesting, but superficial in our first attempts; but the sooner we can produce a material artifact to evaluate, the more we will have to work with. The goal is that we always intend to make things *in order to make them better*. Another way to say this is that in order to really "finish" a project, you will have to produce many "finished" pieces—you have to finish a design a hundred times in order to truly finish it. Design becomes precise when it uses the given criteria and proposed results to sharpen one another. Let

us look at one more example to more fully understand how this process works.

This example also comes from the project mentioned above. In the second instance, a student wanted to create a project that increased awareness of accessibility issues on campus. He identified a particularly long stair as a critical artery for traversing campus. In order to bring awareness of the trials that are encountered daily by disabled individuals, he proposed closing off the stairway using yellow caution tape. Here, again, we see a nice idea with some sound research and analysis, and a reasonable and concrete design response. However, like the student in the previous example, this student also failed to interrogate his own idea further. In short, he saw that it all "made sense," which caused him to be satisfied with the provisional solution he had. However, when pressed for greater precision, he realized that many stairs on campus get blocked off during the winter for snow and ice danger, not to mention that there are several stair locations that are perpetually closed for maintenance-related issues. Further, upon reflection, it began to be unclear how the yellow tape would provide any impetus for those

La Tourette Monastery near Lyon, France, by Le Corbusier.

67

principles of design

As we discussed in the section on play, limits and rules can be incredibly helpful to the designer. Just to prove the point, try to design something by giving yourself only the directive to "make anything you want" or "create something beautiful." Most of us find such lack of direction and definition a very difficult way to begin. In contrast to such freedom, we are usually much better off when we begin by defining what counts and doesn't count within the context of a design: that is, *how* to create something beautiful and *what counts as beauty in this project* are more useful starting points, because they mark out a territory for exploration. For example, beauty is

LIMITS

affected by the closure to reflect upon the trials of those with disabilities: that is, most people would probably just assume the stairs were closed for safety or maintenance issues.

Here, critical reflection upon the effect of the proposed design interventions led to opportunities for greater precision in the next design iteration. Simply, it was exactly because the student made an idea into a concrete design solution that many of the deeper challenges even came to the surface at all. Once the student understood the deficiencies of his preliminary intervention, he was able to go farther and develop several more precise alternate possibilities. For example, barricading the stairway with old wheelchairs was an idea that, through its obtrusive strangeness and recognizability, brought the issue of disabilities to the fore. An intervention like this would not only call attention to the fact that it was not a mere stair closure, but also would offer a material intrusion that communicated a message, as an art piece, in a way that yellow caution tape could not have achieved.

So, in both of these examples, a limited initial solution revealed opportunities and issues that were not apparent in an initial assessment. Here we begin to understand that a large part of creativity is not genius, but rather is simply an attention to detail and a thoroughness in one's interrogation of the design problem. Henri Bergson adds an extra incentive for such effective questioning as he explains, "A speculative problem is solved as soon as it is clearly stated."[33] Deleuze elucidates this insight, saying, "The solution exists then, although it may remain hidden and, so to speak, covered up."[34] This is to say that the questions and interventions direct us more precisely toward what matters in a design problem, and in asking we not only establish that an answer is possible, but in fact capture the answer within the framework of the question itself. This idea is not unlike the relation between *physis* and *techne*; in this case, an answer is waiting for us to "free" it from the situation with the proper question. In this way, a work of design is the product of a search for greater and greater precision in understanding the real depth of the problem and the deficiencies and opportunities in a developing work. Critical thinking is like the sharpening stone of the design project. When we lack precision, we create inappropriate solutions. When we practice precision, we turn our experiments into art.

Design in response to the limits of the natural environment, Mesa Verde, Colorado.

different in a plaza for an office park versus a portrait of the Queen, or even the Queen's garden, for that matter.

principles of design

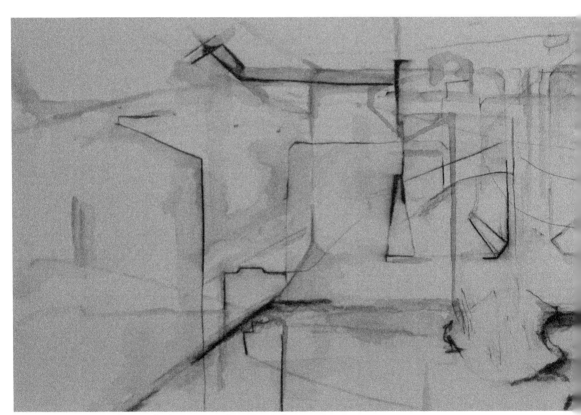

Site intervention vision drawing by first-year student Marc LaPointe.

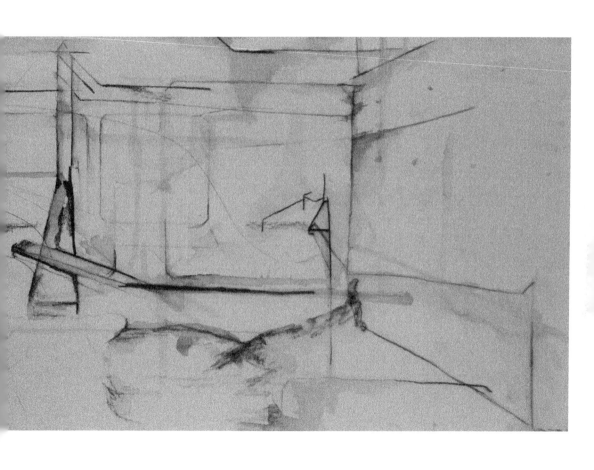

products of design

AFFECT

and sensory experience

"I do not literally paint the table, but the emotion it produces upon me."[1]
Henri Matisse

Affect points to the material specificity of things and how they connect with us via our senses and feelings. We experience affect when we focus on things *as they are* (rather than our definitions of them). Affect shows us that things speak for themselves, regardless of the labels we place upon them, and that this speaking reaches us even before we are conscious of it. Despite the value of affect, relating to people and things solely in terms of affect is challeng-

The Hives live in Barcelona.

Lines have direction. They might be two conjoined points, or they might be made from a compound of points. They can be straight or curved.

LINE

ing; this is because affect is so basic to our experience. Here again, we see our thinking-I taking over feedback that is gleaned through our senses and feelings—the thinking-I does not want us to just leave our experiences at the level of feeling. For example, although one can easily feel affected by, say, the color, texture, loose brushwork, and suggestive forms of a Paul Cézanne painting, we tend to not leave such an encounter at that. Instead, we

"Olympia," Paul Cézanne.

seek to name the artist, look for the painting's title, decipher the subject matter, and analyze the painting in order to understand why it is compelling; and it is through these determinations and judgments that we come to say whether it is "good" or not. Sometimes this kind of understanding is appropriate. The problem is when we completely lose an ability to relate to things affectually.

In conflict with this tendency toward intellectualizing away affect is art itself. Claire Colebrook argues:

> What we *can* acknowledge is that art is not about knowledge, conveying "meanings" or providing information. Art is not just an ornament or style used to make data more palatable or consumable. Art may well have meanings or messages but what makes it *art* is not its content but its *affect*, the sensible force or style through which it produces content.[2]

In other words, art speaks more clearly the less we attempt to label, define, and dissect its messages and meanings.

This is an interesting point, because certainly there can be messages and meaning in artworks. However, what Colebrook is pointing out here is that if art does not work at the level of affect, then it doesn't matter what its content is; and further, art, like our experiences in life, can be

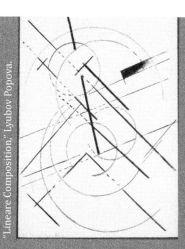

"Lineare Composition," Lyubov Popova.

principles of design

"View of Toledo," El Greco.

it mean?" In fact, these questions would be absurd in this context. Even in an "art" like advertising that is based on conveying messages, it is not uncommon for a different representation of a product to totally change the way we feel about the product—think about all the companies that are now billing their products as environmentally friendly or "green." Further, although it might seem that an advertisement provides you with definite information, often this is not actually the case. Take for example, the famous iPod silhouette ads—there is very little information in these ads, yet many people are simply affected by them and hence drawn to iPods. Here, affect indicates the degree to which art works by involving us emotionally, and this occurs not just visually but through our senses.

The importance of not just treating art and design as being purely visual is critical to understanding how art works. First of all, what the term "visual" usually implies misleads us as to the true nature of vision. We tend to think of vision as a purely detached surveying of the formal quality of things. This misconception comes to us out of the 15th century development of linear measured perspective drawing.

meaningful—affect us—without having any particular meaning. For example, we can be moved by a particular place in nature and never ask, "What is it? What does

The weight and density of a design. Mass can also be literal or perceptual: that is, your sculpture could be made of lead and/or might visually feel heavy. The latter is frequently referred to as *visual weight*, and may occur through differences in color, material, value, position, or shape.

MASS

With this development, there arose a way to accurately measure the distance between the viewpoint and the objects that made up the image, which introduced a mathematical objectivity into our notion of vision. Further, with the establishment of a definite point of view, there became a clear distinction between the viewer and the scene. That is, instead of reinforcing our embodied involvement within certain places, measured perspective afforded the

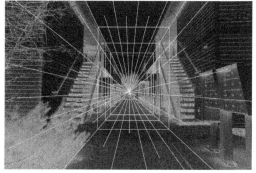

Measured perspective grid.

viewer a position to look upon, or into, the context, from the outside. In contrast to a notion of vision that is based upon detached formal description, closer analysis of the way vision works tells us that our sense of sight is not merely for superficial

description, but rather is an extension of our sense of touch. Finnish architect Juhani Palasmaa wrote a wonderful book about this strange, often unrealized aspect of vision, called *The Eyes of the Skin*. In this book he points out:

> Vision reveals what the touch already knows. We could think of the sense of touch as the unconscious of vision. Our *eyes* stroke distant surfaces, contours and edges, and the unconscious tactile sensation determines the agreeableness or unpleasantness of the experience. The distant and the near are experienced with the same intensity, and they merge into one coherent experience.[3]

So, the idea here is that when we look at things, we are actually extending our sense of touch. When you look at a piece of metal, you feel its coldness. When you look at a piece of wood, you feel its warmth. When you look at a brick wall, you feel its roughness. When you look at a flower, you feel its delicacy. This occurs because these objects literally exist in this way and our sense of touch can experience this as an aspect of our seeing. Here, affect is this resonance of these encounters; it is in this way that

principles of design

The bell tower and entry have a greater sense of mass than the stained glass window. St. John's Abbey by Marcel Breuer, Collegeville, Minnesota.

our bodies become vital instruments of our understanding.

This embodied aspect of affect goes even further when you think about the environment. In the environment, we are always in space. That is, we are enmeshed within places and situations that surround us (i.e., we are not standing outside looking in), and our bodies register differences in their spatial qualities. Think about standing in a closet versus standing in an auditorium—there is a very distinct difference in terms of how your body feels. Further, our bodies can also feel our proximity to an object in space. Stand so that you are close to an ob-

Media in design designates the types of material you are using in your work: pencil, pen, paint, bronze, wood, paper, canvas, etc.

ject but not looking directly at it. You will be able to feel the weight or pressure of the object, and, in contrast, you will be able to sense the openness of the area that is not occupied by this object. A primal version of this kind of haptic sense is called prospect and refuge, which speaks to our preference for having our backs protected while we look out onto a space (imagine sitting at the mouth of a cave looking over the valley and how this compares to sitting on the front porch of one's house). We sense that we are protected and thus free to survey the open in front of us. However, the importance of our senses to our understandings goes beyond vision and touch alone.

Being able to relate to this embodied being-in-space is crucial for designers, because it recognizes how important multisensory understanding is to our feelings about things, people, and places and thus encourages the incorporation of such understanding into our design. Palasmaa uses an example from Kakuzo Okakura's *The Book of Tea* to illustrate the full multisensory impact of the world around us:

> In *The Book* of *Tea* Kakuzo Okakura gives a fine description of the multisensory imagery evoked by the simple experi-
ence of the tea ceremony: "quiet reigns with nothing to break the silence save the note of the boiling water in the iron kettle. The kettle sings well, for pieces of iron are so arranged in the bottom as to produce a peculiar melody in which one may hear the echoes of a cataract muffled by clouds, of a distant sea breaking among the rocks, a rainstorm sweeping through a bamboo forest, or of the soughing of pines on some faraway hill." In Okakura's description the present and the absent, the near and the distant, the sensed and the imagined fuse together. The body is not a mere physical entity; it is enriched by both memory and dream. The world is reflected in the body, and the body is projected on the world.

Although they are not mentioned in this passage, you can also imagine the smell and taste of the tea as being critical aspects of the whole of this experience. So it is that the things of the world affect us through our senses, and we can simply feel joy, warmth, coldness, fear, sadness, wonder, and so on, by allowing things to be as they are—without labels and judgments. Such affective phenomena can also draw us into participation and action.

MOOD and *WORLD*

"America, how can I write a holy litany in your silly mood?"[4]
Allen Ginsberg

Like affect, mood alerts us to the fact that our interaction with the world is always already affecting us. However, in the awareness of mood, we find that we develop understandings as well. In other words, mood highlights how the things we do are often the result of a feeling, rather than an explicitly conscious decision. Further, mood is pervasive, something one is immersed in; perhaps the real experience of mood is betrayed by the colloquial "I'm *in* a _____ mood." In this way, mood is like the weather, and the whole of one's involvements show

BVB Dortmund soccer fans being moved to action by the mood of the match.

Modeling is a technique in drawing that gives the illusion of three-dimensionality through the use of shade and shadow.

MODELING

up in the light of this mood. For example, when the mood is "sunny," things take on a sunny tinge.

Ultimately, mood is not concerned with the individual objects or details; rather, mood is concerned with the collective—the context and the relationships therein. In this way, we see how mood is related to world: that is, it addresses the wholeness of our encounters. Hubert Dreyfus explains:

> Mood can refer to the sensibility of an age (such as romantic), the culture of a company (such as aggressive), the temper of the times (such as revolutionary), as well as the mood in a current situation (such as the eager mood in the classroom) and, of course, the mood of an individual. These are all ways of finding that things matter.

As Dreyfus says, mood orients us to what matters in a given situation, and it does this pre-cognitively.

These understandings are exemplified in, and augmented by, our use of tools. First, certain tools only become relevant in certain situations—you pull out your pen to draw something in class, but not to eat din-

Finnish kids swept up in the mood of a Joan Jett concert.

ner. Second, using a pen effectively depends upon not focusing on the pen itself, but on whatever it is that we are drawing. Finally, the pen is already interconnected with such things as paper, ink, a studio desk, perhaps other design media like charcoal and graphite, and so on. This web of relations and the whole that they are a part of are critical to the way we perceive situations. Here, again, the interplay between the whole and the particular is critical, and we perceive this interdependence even if we are in an unknown circumstance. Heidegger explains:

> Even in the workshop of a craftsman whose craft is totally unfamiliar to us is

"Adamo," Michelangelo Buonarroti.

81

principles of design

in no way first encountered as a mere conglomerate of things scattered in disarray. Manifest in the immediate orientation of preoccupation are hand tools, material, manufactured finished pieces, unfinished items in process. What we primarily experience is the world in which the man lives. Even though it is strange, it is still experienced as a world, as a closed totality of references.[5]

As Heidegger says in the passage, this kind of referential whole is what he calls "world," and he uses "world" to describe the interdependence between our perceiving the parts and understanding the whole of the context that occurs in any situation. Further, world indicates that within this implicit set of relations there are behavioral possibilities that open up for us. That is, we know what to do in certain worlds: we listen to lectures in classrooms, we drink coffee in coffee shops—and we know what not to do: we do not play tennis in history class, we do not bathe in coffee shops. Importantly, we perform all these understandings without having to become consciously aware that we understand, and we perform such understandings constantly. In this way, "world," for the most part, is only explicitly acknowledged when something breaks down within it. For example, when the soccer ball goes flat during a match, the web of relations ruptures and everyone becomes very aware of what is needed for an active soccer match.

Further, it is not just that we become aware of the opportunities and prohibitions of a world, but that we also respond spontaneously. For example, at a concert people will naturally begin to dance, clap, and sing along, but they tend *not to* dance, clap, or

The idea of narrative is relevant to design because it points to the need for using a language of experience and not just a language of technique when we design. In other words, the need for functionality in design can often push people to try to understand it (and practice it) from a perspective of reason and pure mathematical precision. As we discussed in the body of the book, this limited perspective skews our work away from our humanity.

Narrative is the language of humanity, and thinking through a design as one might create a story (either in prose or poems) is critical to the designer's engagement with and activation of

NARRATIVE

sing along when attending a physics lecture or going out to dinner. Mood is the affective practical aspect of world and highlights gross difference (between a coffee shop and a classroom) as well as more subtle differences. For instance, following the concert example, it is easy to see that the world of a rock concert is different than that of a classical concert. In the world of classical music, everyone applauds the conductor's arrival, but when the music starts there is silence. Further, one does not clap after a

other aspect of how world is articulated through mood functions—people who clap at the wrong time quickly begin to behave "properly" because of the publicness of the experience: that is, one immediately feels that they clapped at the wrong time, and curtails such future behavior. Mood is even further nuanced beyond the obvious categorical difference in mood between a rock concert and classical concert. The worlds of, say, a Pink Floyd concert, a Grateful Dead concert, and a Green Day concert are all

The world of a rock concert (Jane's Addiction) versus the world of a classical concert.

movement within a classical work, despite the fact that all the musicians stop playing at that point; applause comes at the end of the entire work. Interestingly, this idiosyncrasy of classical decorum shows us an-

very different, and within them we first feel difference as a mood. All individuals will experience this mood slightly differently and respond accordingly.

life of the people that will populate a work. Think about how much the stories of Charles Dickens depend upon the city of London, or how the landscape of the Mediterranean shapes the tales of Homer. Narrative understandings of your design work allow it to weave together people and the places in which they exist.

principles of design

Different rock concert worlds (clockwise from top left): Lady Gaga, Lenny Kravitz, Kiss, and Shakira.

the importance of
THINGS

"Things congeal the places we remember, just as places congeal remembered worlds."[6]
Edward Casey

For designers, what is important about these affective phenomena is that they both begin and end with things: which is to say that, as important as other people are to our existence, our various worlds of involvement are structured and made possible by things like buildings, chairs, lec-

In addition to mere proximity, which designates objective physical closeness in space, Heidegger suggested that we also experience a kind of existential "nearness" in our dealing with the world. In this phenomenon, something that is physically far away from you might be experienced as more significant to you than something else that is very close by. This sense of significance is nearness. Imagine you are working on something. Now imagine that you wear eyeglasses. In this experience, the thing you are working on will be "nearer" to you than your eyeglasses; that is,

NEARNESS

terns, stoves, shelves, desks, etc. Things provide both a particular aesthetic (affect) and particular opportunities for involvement (mood).

Important to the products of art is the difference between a "thing" and an object. That is to say, the material stuff of our world can exist in a primarily inert and quantitative way (object) or in a way that has force (thing). The latter comes about via a dual movement. A thing may have force because of its distinctive or wholly integral material presence, or by way of our

mindfulness of them. Usually, this occurs through some combination of both.

This is an important difference for artists and designers to be aware of, because it indicates the dual movement that is design. That is, a designer must be attentive so that the material world can be seen in its specific force, and must also strive to create things that help to facilitate this awareness in others. When things have affective power, an energetic interplay occurs—a "thing-thinging," as Heidegger calls it; and when a thing "things," events take shape.

When an event takes shape, we find that some things support and frame, while others become focal. To understand the differing roles of things, we return to the classical concert example once more. In this situation, the seats, the stage, the lighting, the hall itself, all these things perform by becoming unobtrusive—they form the basic infrastructure of the event. This type of thing is the same as the tools we talked about earlier; for a pen to perform as a pen it cannot be obtrusive. So it is too with these other types of equipment.

"Things" congealing a place, Whitefish, Montana.

A focal thing is the point of gathering for an event. In a concert, these would probably

The shoe is "nearer" to the shoemaker than his glasses. "Shoemaker," Jefferson David Chalfant.

you will feel the work is closer to you than your glasses (which, if they are working properly, you shouldn't even be aware of).

The importance of nearness is related to the importance of narrative, in that nearness too describes an important part of how we experience and understand our world that cannot be served by purely instrumental means.

principles of design

"Things" congealing a place, Pittsburgh, Pennsylvania.

Negative space is the emptiness around any object or collection of objects. In art and design, focus on this space around objects can (a) help you draw the objects better, because it presents their form from a slightly different perspective, which can help to clarify their nuances, and (b) help strengthen compositions. Designing the negative space around an object or series of objects can help to clarify and strengthen the cohesion of the piece. When the negative space has a discernible presence, some have called this a figural void—meaning an emptiness that has a presence like an object.

NEGATIVE SPACE

be the musical instruments. Let's say that we are going to listen to a solo piano performance. Before the pianist comes on stage, the audience is not focused on the piano that is sitting on the stage—the concert has not begun and thus a piano is not yet a focal thing. However, as the pianist begins to play, the interaction between pianist and piano brings the classical concert into sharp focus. As the audience becomes part of this focus, other concerns fall away. Here, the thing can be said to be properly "thinging." In other words, a thing-thinging is this whole of this event we call a concert, where, for a short amount of time, there is a synthesis of pianist, piano, and audience. The affective qualities of the things help to structure the event and to set the mood: that is, the look, feel, performance, and particular orientation things provide to the concert are what allow this event to take place at all.

In this example, the variety of roles a designed object might play is underlined, providing another reminder about the necessity of precision in our design thinking. For example, it is interesting to note that in this context a well-designed chair is one that facilities listening; in other words, a seat that is attractive but not demonstrative, com-

fortable but not sumptuous. Designing stylishly super-plush lounge chairs for this venue would be inappropriate for a variety of reasons. Aside from cost and a need to fit a reasonable number of seats in the hall, chairs that are too unique and too comfortable would divert the focus of an audience member who should not be thinking about

Concert hall, La Jolla, California.

the seats, but should be engaged in the performance itself. It is this kind of particular definition that design is always concerned with; and in this way, good design is never absolute, but is relative to the task at hand.

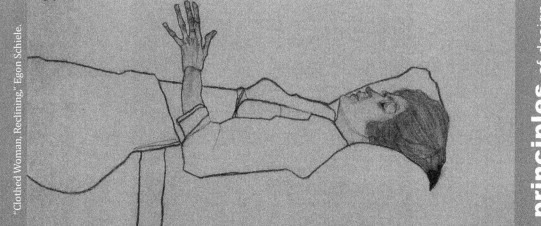

"Clothed Woman, Reclining," Egon Schiele.

principles of design

MATTER and FORM

"Forms in art arise from the impact of idea upon material . . . so that thinking and belief and attitudes may endure as actual things."[7]

Ben Shahn

As designers, it is important that we understand how things are made, and how what those things are made of affects their presence, character, and effect. In talking about the things of the earth, Aristotle developed a theory of hylomorphism; that is, he theorized that the particularity of things is born out of the interdependence of form and matter.

Matter refers to the substance of things, or what they are made of, like wood, clay, canvas, or paper, but also might refer to the words that make up a book. Matter can be both proximate and non-proximate. By proximate, we mean proximity—how close something is—and this reflects the fact that the substance of a thing can have nested levels. For example, the walls of a building might be covered in sheetrock panels, yet these panels are made of gypsum. So, proximally, the sheetrock is closer to being a room than the gypsum, which is one step removed.

An orthographic projection is a two-dimensional drawing that represents some aspect of a three-dimensional thing. Typical varieties of orthographic drawings are plans, sections, and elevations. This type of drawing is used quite frequently in the design disciplines, and usually a combination of these drawings will appear simultaneously as a means of describing a more complex entity or phenomenon.

ORTHOGRAPHIC

Form is what the end of the raw material is. For example, wood can be made into a bench, a chair, a table, or a house (to name a few). Further, as we discussed above, there could be a whole host of different types of tables that could be made. In this way, form can be understood in both general categories and specific ends within these categories.

To put all this simply, matter is potential and form is actuality. However, it is important to bear in mind that the two can never be separated: matter is always realized in some form, and form is made particular by the specific types of matter that make it up.

Connected to this theory of hylomorphism is Aristotle's principle of "four causes." This principle is a description of how change occurs. The four causes are the material cause, the formal cause, the efficient cause, and the final cause. When we make things, we are constantly bringing these four causes together. Let us use a coffee mug as an example. Here we will look at the final cause first, because this cause tells us about a thing's end. In this case, the end for a coffee cup is to hold and ultimately allow one to drink coffee: its purpose is to drink coffee. The material cause goes along with the fact that coffee is a hot drink, and in this case it is ceramic. The formal cause is the particular forms that synthesize this

A Zen garden at Kodaiji Temple, Kyoto, Japan.

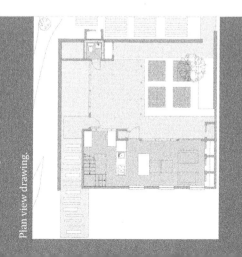

Plan view drawing.

Three sizes of coffee available at Thomas Hammer Coffee, Pullman, Washington.

particular combination of end and material. That is, a coffee mug cannot be 60 feet tall because its end is for humans to drink coffee, and it cannot have walls that are 1/32" thick because the material would not allow this. Further, this mug might have different ends if, let's say, a coffee house were to serve different sized drinks. Here, a 12-ounce drink, a 16-ounce drink, and a 20-ounce drink would each demand a different form in order to accommodate the volume of liquid they were to contain. Lastly, the efficient cause points to the designer and/or manufacturer that brings these mugs into existence and the certain choices they make in designing the look of these mugs.

Pattern is a way to think about aesthetics without relying upon meaning, understanding, or identifiability. Many types of design such as quilts, rugs, and tribal art rely on pattern as a primary means of expression. Pattern is a technique based in repetition and rhythm and can be used to create movement, continuity, and dynamics in a work.

Pattern can also refer to the built environment, where we talk of "patterns of life" or "settlement patterns." Here, pattern can help us think about the rhythms of the city and archetypes of dwelling.

PATTERN

truth, strife, and the
SHINING OF ART

"The truth must dazzle gradually / Or every man be blind."[8]
Emily Dickinson

In a famous essay, "The Origin of the Work of Art," Heidegger spoke of an inherent tension in a work of art. This tension occurs because of what he calls a "strife" between "earth" and "world." This description of a work of art is helpful for our understanding of what is present in a good design, and it orients us to the fact that we simultaneously perceive what an artwork is (world) and how it is made (earth). These two parts are loosely connected to Aristotle's form and material. However, Heidegger takes this distinction further by broadening the factors these terms (form and matter) encompass.

We know about Heidegger's concept of world from the earlier section on this topic. Accordingly, world here does not just refer to the form of the object, but also to how

A bodhisattva carved in wood, Nara, Japan.

the object connects to its surroundings —how it opens up a world. Similarly, earth is not just raw materials, but how these

Parking area/garden, Baton Rouge, Louisiana.

principles of design

"Venezia, Canal Grande," Antonio Canaletto.

As we discussed above, world is the wholeness of the work, but it is a whole that communicates something more extensive and ambiguous than what we might say something like a painting "represents." For example, take a painting of Venice by Antonio Canaletto. Here, there is a clear representative likeness of the actualities of Venice that one can recognize and define, and this representation could be thought of as the whole of the artwork, but Heidegger wants us to go further. He asks not only that we see what is present in the representation, but that we are transported by the representation into the time, place, and culture that that work is situated within. So, in addition to the actualities of the scene that are being shown, we also have hints of values, activities, and material and social sensibilities of this time and place. In this fashion, the painting suggests not just the moment that was painted, but the greater world that these people inhabit. For example, there is the suggestion of what it would be like to live in a city whose primary transportation is waterborne; and perhaps more interesting as we look down

materials are understood when they are in use. And, most importantly, through the notion of "strife," Heidegger drives home the importance of the interplay of these two factors. That is, earth and world do not add together arithmetically: they multiply each other. In this way, the strife between "earth" and "world" describes the peculiar power of a work of art, which stems from the tension between its impact as a whole and the specific affect of its craft—that is, what it is and how it is made, and how these two combine to affect us. In order to make it easier to understand the strife, let us first get clear about earth and world more explicitly.

A drawing type that provides the illusion of three-dimensional space on a two-dimensional surface. It is characterized by lines that converge toward a vanishing point or points (there are three types: "one-point," "two-point," and "three-point" perspective), and foreshortening—an effect where objects or distances appear shorter than they actually are.

Perspective was developed systematically during the Italian Renaissance into a system that could be mathematically constructed and used to represent (and measure) distances accurately.

PERSPECTIVE

that canal at the uniformity of the black gondolas, we understand there is a very different notion about what a thing of use (boat) should be.

Compared to our contemporary world, where we expect variety in the things and goods of the world, these boats do not speak of the personalization and customization we are so accustomed to. And, in spite of the fact that Venice has kept the traditional black gondolas alive, modern Venice is a different place than the Venice that Canaletto painted, because it is punctuated by the variety we have come to expect. Yet, there is still a "Venice" that persists in both, inasmuch as it has been able to accommodate the changes that we have observed. If this example reminds you of Heraclitus' aphorism about not being able to step in the same river twice—it should. Heidegger's point here is that the work of art finds its greatest potency as it reveals things about the world beyond its boundaries while finding wholeness in its own right through its material specificity.

To make this point about the reach of the artwork clearer, let us think now of non-

A contemporary view of the Grand Canal, Venice, Italy.

representational art. Heidegger refers to a Greek temple as a work of art that does not represent or refer to anything else, and has a sense of wholeness as a temple. Yet, this wholeness is not just as a recognizable building type, but more importantly as a particular entity: for example, the Parthenon, the Hephaestion, or the Temple of Poseidon.

And yet its worth as a work of art does not merely end as a beautiful building: for the Greeks, a temple also embodies and reflects certain aspects of their culture and place. For example, the fact that each temple was dedicated to an individual god both supports and reveals the pantheism of their

"Perspective Drawing for the Pair-Oared Shell," Thomas Eakins.

society; and the fact that different gods were tied to different types of places points to the link between their spirituality and particular locations (the Greeks had no word for space, only place [*topos*]). In this

that when a work of art is "working," it can make concrete those things that are meaningful and significant within that culture. Another example of an artwork working in this way is a medieval cathedral. In its time, it would have stood above the town reminding everyone of the highest power in their lives; the cathedral would have literally gathered the local Christian populace and facilitated their understanding and practice of the primary meaning of their existence—Christianity.

The Parthenon, Athens, Greece.

way, the Parthenon, let's say, can be both a beautiful building and the epitome of a culture. Regarding the latter, as was alluded to earlier, Heidegger claimed that a work of art opens up a world. What he means is

Such working can be seen in great civic works like temples and cathedrals, but it may also be seen in a more humble work like Pieter de Hooch's painting "A Boy Bringing Pomegranates." In this painting, the activities and values of a certain way of life in a particular place and time are captured in the simple exchange between the woman and boy and their surroundings.

Now let us return to the other player in this strife: earth. In thinking about earth, it is

Phenomenology is a philosophical movement that began in the early part of the twentieth century. Its focus was to try to describe the world as it is and how we operate within it, rather than trying to explain it. One driving question for phenomenology was not what an object was, but instead how it affects us. In this way it was an attempt to break free of the rationalizing tradition of Western philosophy and, as such, it opened an important avenue for design theory.

PHENOMENOLOGY

Nôtre Dame Cathedral, Paris, France.

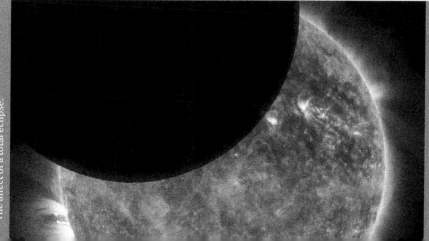

The affect of a total eclipse.

"A Boy Bringing Pomegranates," Pieter de Hooch.

Place speaks of our ability to recognize and connect with the identity of specific locations. And, in fact, we experience a place's specific identity *before* we can think of it as just a volume—a space. In other words, place is not identity added to space, it is the fundamental condition of our encounters—we always find ourselves "placed" within the world.

There are natural places like the ocean that are comprised of very specific material things, as well as constructed places like schools, parks, and homes that are also made of very particular material things. Further, place can refer to an exalted identity, like Stonehenge,

first important to remember that earth does not refer to just inert physical material; rather, it talks about how the material stuff around us often has a tendency to elude direct scientific scrutiny in terms of understanding significance, beauty, and potential, and is often better understood when it is put into use. For example, asking what a rock or air *is* naturally leads to the definitions and categories of science. Heidegger explains:

A stone presses downward and manifests its heaviness. But while this heaviness exerts an opposing pressure upon us it denies us any penetration into it. If we attempt such a penetration by breaking open the rock, it still does not display in its fragments anything inward that has been disclosed. The stone has instantly withdrawn again into the same dull pressure and bulk of its fragments. If we try to lay hold of the stone's heaviness in another way, by placing the stone on a balance, we merely bring the heaviness into the form of a calculated weight. This perhaps very precise determination of the stone remains a number, but the weight's burden has escaped us . . . Earth thus shatters every attempt to penetrate into it. It causes every merely calculating importunity upon it to turn into a destruction.[9]

As the Herman Melville quote early in the book described trying to understand the "living contour" of the whale, when we seek explanations by measuring, weighing, and breaking down, we fail to grasp the holistic significance of the item of inquiry. Certainly, such explorations are useful in the right context; however, the answers of science do not satisfy our human desire for meaning. This is why art and earth are connected; art's very domain is that of the significance of particular circumstances and interventions and those things that might be called ineffable. Earth is important to the "working" of the artwork because it is the material-craft that we immediately perceive when experiencing a work of art, and is exactly what allows the work to transcend general categories. That is, it is the specific, say, horse that has been painted and the way it has been painted that is remarkable, not the identification of the general category of the subject matter.

The truth that we are pursuing in this current discussion is not a scientific "truth,"

Bern, Switzerland.

or to more common identities, like the place where I keep my jacket.

principles of design

In these five different representations of horses, it is the specifics that matter. The images in this figure, clockwise from the left are: "Cavalier Écossais," Gustave Moreau; "Prince of Wales Phaeton," George Stubbs; "Monfa conduisant son mail," Henri de Toulouse-Lautrec; "Lady Thorn," Currier and Ives; and on the opposite page "The Jockey," Henri de Toulouse-Lautrec.

A plane is a basic closed form. It can be defined by lines (an outline) or points (a field or array), or might be an area that has been shaded or hatched. A plane is the basic means of distinguishing one area from another.

PLANE

like the fact that the atomic number of gold is 79. Instead, we are interested in the kind of "truth" that is revealed when we discover that gold is a unique material for, say, metalsmiths to craft things from. That is to say, there is a different kind of truth that is revealed in the remarkable malleability and ductility of gold—a gram of gold can be beaten into a one-square-meter sheet—than the truths that number and measure tend to bring us. Here, truth equals the revelation that gold offers amazing possibilities for making things; it speaks to its singular uniqueness as a material as revealed by particular contexts.

This notion of truth was known to the Greeks as *aletheia*—Heidegger called it "uncoveredness"—and what this term highlights is the fact that we often "uncover" more about a material or object when we deploy it in a specific context for a particular purpose than when we try to define or explain it as such. *Aletheia* highlights the fact that we uncover a truth about, say, a certain type of stone when it is used as a roof to keep the weather out of your house; and that this "information" is not a

A plane differentiating one part of the garden from another at Ginkakuji Temple, Kyoto, Japan.

universal property of all stone, but is a situational property of this particular stone. Taking this example a little further, let us imagine that we tried to roof the same house with basalt or river rock. We would probably find these kinds of stone were unsuitable to the task. However, in their failure as roofing material, they too, according to *aletheia*, would reveal something basic about their nature—they are good for things *other than roofing*. Finally, this stone roof makes a lot of sense in this traditional Swiss village, but probably less so on an American suburban tract house or a big-city apartment building.

The kind of truth revealed in historical examples is useful in coming to understand the concept of strife between earth and world, and how this strife makes a work of art different than more utilitarian designs. The difference is that the latter does not have the "strife" of earth and world. Instead, the material in a utilitarian design tends to settle into the whole of the design, which allows things like roofs, shoes, drinking glasses, and other types of tools to recede from our consciousness: that is, we tend to use these things without them arresting our activity through our awareness of their presence. For instance, like the pen we learned about in a previous section, the stone in the roofing example also works best the more it becomes inconspicuously incorporated into the assembly of the house. In other words, if the roofing stone becomes too self-important, it runs the risk of destroying the integrity of the whole, which is comprised of a variety of parts and other materials. One can see this inappropriate competitiveness of parts in many less than stellar contemporary examples.

In contrast to the inconspicuousness of the material in utilitarian objects, the material of a work of art "shines": the singular presence of the material itself becomes conspicuous as it is amplified by the whole of the work of art—the pragmatic implementation of stone in a utilitarian structure versus the elaborately carved stone of a cathedral. In this way, a work of art seeks to arrest everyday consciousness and remind us about things beyond our everyday tasks.

Historically, this arresting often had to do with a kind of higher-order. For example, the Greeks saw this higher-order in the ex-

Plastic speaks not to a material, but to the fact that our life, art, and designs are constantly forming and reforming around us. The world is fluid in this way, and at any moment, one can come to recognize something remarkable just to have it dissolve into something else. The acknowledgment of the plastic nature of life and its formings and reformings allows time to become effectual in our work.

PLASTIC

istence of universal principles amid the flux of nature (*physis*); for the Romans this higher-order was the glory of Rome itself; and for medieval Christians it was God and his promise of an eternal life beyond the hardships of the Middle Ages. In each of

Stone roofs in Vals, Switzerland.

"Cubo-futurist Composition," Kazimir Malevich.

principles of design

these examples, viewers would have been simultaneously moved by the overall presence of the work (world) and the shining of the material/workmanship that made up its specific material presence (earth).

To better understand what Heidegger means by strife, and to begin to imagine how it might be relevant to our current artistic endeavors, let us look at several small-scale examples. First, a drawing from

A vernacular stone building in Glacier National Park.

A point is the most basic mark one can make. A single point can be complicated by adding a second point, implying a line. Multiple points can begin to suggest shapes and forms; clusters of points can indicate groups and have density. In the late 1800s, the pointillist painters Georges Seurat and Paul Signac even went so far as to create huge colored canvases made up only of points.

POINT

Edgar Degas: in this drawing there is a perceptual tension between the power of the image as a whole and the virtuosity of his technique, which catalyzes a transformation of mere lines, dots, and scribbles placed on paper into a shining material construction.

In the strife, the viewer's attention is pulled between the beauty of the dancer as a

Carved stone at Pisa Cathedral.

"River Landscape with a Boat", Georges Seurat.

principles of design

whole and the shining affect of its various virtuosic moments.

"Dancer," Edgar Degas.

Another example of this productive tension can be seen in a different material—words. Let us return to Melville's *Moby Dick,* which is a compelling story about the battle between Captain Ahab and the white whale. However, it isn't just the idea of the story that makes it compelling, it is also *the way it is written*. For example:

> All that most maddens and torments; all that stirs up the lees of things; all truth with malice in it; all that cracks the sinews and cakes the brain; all the subtle demonisms of life and thought; all evil, to crazy Ahab, were visibly personified, and made practically assailable in Moby-Dick. He piled upon the whale's white hump the sum of all the general rage and hate felt by his whole race from Adam down; and then, as if his chest had been a mortar, he burst his hot heart's shell upon it.[10]

In this example, one's attention can be on the bigger notion of the story, the beauty of the language, or both. The notion of strife means that we tend to oscillate between the two, neither one winning, each strengthening the other. This is what happens in a work of art. For clarity, let us examine a counterexample—*Angels and Demons* by Dan Brown. Now, this too is an intriguing story, about a guy trying to solve a murder and prevent a terrorist act; how-

We have an ability to sense our own bodies in space. This happens unconsciously and goes on constantly. This helps us maintain our balance, walk down stairs without looking at the stairs explicitly, and put food in our mouths (you must know where your hand is in relation to your face to perform this operation). Proprioception is one of our many embodied intelligences.

PROPRIOCEPTION

ever, it is filled with clichés, mediocre prose, and awkward dialogue. For example:

"Do you have children, Lieutenant?"

Chartrand flushed. "No, signore."

"Imagine you had an eight-year-old son ... would you love him?"

"Of course."

"Would you let him skateboard?"

Chartrand did a double take. The camerlengo always seemed oddly "in touch" for a clergyman. "Yeah, I guess," Chartrand said. "Sure, I'd let him skateboard, but I'd tell him to be careful."

"So as this child's father, you would give him some basic, good advice and then let him go off and make his own mistakes?"

"I wouldn't run behind him and mollycoddle him if that's what you mean."

"But what if he fell and skinned his knee?"

"He would learn to be more careful."

The camerlengo smiled. "So although you have the power to interfere and prevent your child's pain, you would choose to show your love by letting him learn his own lessons?"

"Of course. Pain is part of growing up. It's how we learn."

The camerlengo nodded. "Exactly."[11]

This conversation is a not-so-subtle lesson given in not-so-elegant language. The lack of quality in the writing leads to ruptures in your attention. Instead of being rapt by the story, we are thrust out of the illusion by a lack of craft. As much as *Angels and Demons* might be an intriguing story, it is not a work of art—details matter.

empowering
DETAILS

"God is in the details."[12]
Mies van der Rohe

The precision of critical thinking, discussed earlier, is concerned with the specific "fit" of a design and the way the development of its details is the essential point of finish for a work. "World" details involve the forces and practices that are more temporal and circumstantial, like the fact that a society is agrarian, pantheistic, or maternal. Here, details such as climate, local ecology, cultural mores, and technological developments have a role in shaping the work

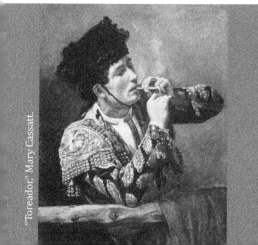

"Toreador," Mary Cassatt.

A perfect concrete stair banister, Chur, Switzerland.

tural and ecological filters; these filters allow certain types of work to occur and preclude others from even being possible. Take, for example, the emergence of jazz as a musical form in the 1800s. It is not unimportant that jazz grew up in New Orleans. As Ken Burns describes in his series *Jazz*, New Orleans was at the turn of the 19th century a place where the lives of a wide range of people with different backgrounds and musical sensibilities collided: there were Africans, former slaves from the Caribbean, others from the north that were steeped in work songs, and Southern Baptists who engaged in the spirituals and call-and-response of the Baptist church; additionally there were Europeans and a unique group of people called Creoles of color, who were descendants of mixed racial backgrounds (European, black, Native American), both of which often had classical music training. Burns goes on to describe how this wide range of people was complemented by the popular entertainments of the time—minstrel shows, the blues, brass bands, and the emerging ragtime music. New Orleans drew together the heterogeneity of these various influences and ultimately allowed them to coalesce as jazz.[13]

(alongside the artist), and may be revealed through the work (i.e., Inuits do not build mud-brick dwellings for good reason). In other words, details like these do not emerge explicitly nor are they imagined into being, but they emerge through cul-

Proportion is a key principle because it highlights the importance of the relationships between things. Proportion addresses the relative sizes of things, and in design points to the fact that most often it is this relative size, not absolute size, that is most consequential to a work's sense of finish. For example, the Roman architect Marcus Vitruvius Pollio came up with a set of "rules" about classical architecture based on the proportion of certain parts in relation to other parts and how getting these proportions correct was ultimately the critical avenue toward the integrity of the entire work. During

PROPORTION

Continuing with this example, we can also see the importance of earth details. In jazz, earth details begin with the instruments themselves and their particular sounds—jazz would be very different if it were developed on the instruments of the Indonesian gamelan. Brass instruments in particular form a very important aspect of the jazz sound. However, simply forcing air through a cornet is not music, and further, someone playing musical notes on a cornet is not necessarily playing jazz; finally, jazz cannot be just thought of as a general category, *it is* its specific interpretations. Here, it becomes apparent that earth details allow for, and perhaps demand, individual creativity much more then world details. In the development of jazz, the role of the players themselves is apparent. The sheer force of a Buddy Bolton, the lyricism of a Sidney Bechet, or the unabashed genius of a Louis Armstrong; all these players point to the importance of individual creativity (and skill) to this art form.

In fact, the impact of individuals on earth details is a common theme throughout art and design. From the virtuoso treatment of marble and paint respectively found in Ber-

The French Quarter, New Orleans, Louisiana.

nini and Caravaggio, to the less conventional brushstrokes of a Van Gogh or De Kooning, to the technological inventions of a Jenny Holzer or John Maeda, it is apparent that there is a distinctive impact that both the particularities of material and an

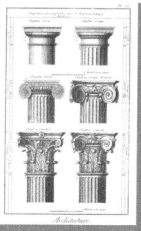

The classical orders of architecture.

the French Enlightenment, a number of architects sought to make this system more predictable and moved to turn these relative proportions into absolute values. In this transformation they destroyed the true understanding of the classical system, which was necessarily uncertain and based on interpretation.

In application, focusing on questions of proportion is a way to balance your work. That is, thinking about your work from the perspective of proportion allows the various parts of a project to speak and relate to one another.

principles of design

individual's creativity have in crafting the pure affective material presence of any work.

However, it is important to remember that neither earth details nor world details alone make a work of art: both must be effectual. That is, there must be two different types of significance existing simultaneously in the work. To make art and design that achieves this kind of tension, an artist must have a high aptitude for the kind of listening discussed earlier in the book as well as a mastery of his or her craft; these skills allow world details to emerge and earth details to both reinforce this whole and shine on their own. A wonderful example of such sensitivity and skill is the Italian architect Carlo Scarpa.

Scarpa practiced architecture toward the latter end of the 20th century and is famous for his detailing. His project in Verona, Castelvecchio, provides an instructive demonstration of these skills. Castelvecchio is the adaptive reuse of an old fortification that transforms it into an art museum. In doing this project, Scarpa was supremely aware of the value of the old building; however, this did not lead him to attempt to preserve it as is, or simply try to restore it to some kind of past glory. Instead, what Scarpa did was to carefully and intentionally make his interventions and modifications find a new integrated relationship with the old structure, allowing the world details of the old structure to both be present and to guide his new interventions. He achieved this, in part, not by making the new pieces look like the old pieces, but rather by devising an ensemble of parts that translated the general spirit of the place into a modern language. He did this by using a fairly limited palette of materials (steel, concrete, and wood), and a minimalist approach in his detailing; in this project, he seemingly asked all of his details to amplify details of the existing structure and the artworks housed within. The important point about this project is that Scarpa did not show his respect for the old structure by creating a design that worked by

Design details at Castelvecchio by Carlo Scarpa, Verona, Italy.

Paths woven through Castelvecchio (above) and the crossing with the equestrian statue.

"disappearing" into the old castle; instead, he created a design that used the existing condition as a springboard. In this way, the whole of the new place might be said to be better than the existing place, because it adds layers of interest to this place. In Castelvecchio, this layering culminates in a singular moment of high drama in the building, which occurs in the joint between the two main buildings. Here a panoply of pedestrian paths intersect and stack vertically, and serve to transport the visitor past a famous equestrian statue that is cantilevered out over the void. This project is one of the strongest examples of how to design so that the whole and its details enter into a dynamic tension. This tension, one that plays out over and over again in great works of art, is a relationship that is simultaneously a competition and a cooperation.

art and design in a
CONSUMER
CULTURE

"Have nothing in your house that you do not know to be useful, or believe to be beautiful."[14]
William Morris

Trinkets for sale outside a Buddhist shrine, Kyoto, Japan.

encompassing, world-defining type of art becomes impossible as cultures become more heterogeneous. In other words, it would be difficult to imagine a contemporary example that so wholly defined a culture and place the way a Greek temple or Medieval cathedral might be seen to do. This is, in part, because our existence on this planet is shaped by a global scale and connectivity.

Despite the different world we inhabit, there remains this tension between the whole and the specific material craft that drives art and the interplay between the work and its world. That is to say, even though there are few cultures with the intense similarity of beliefs and practices of, say, the medieval Christians, where a work like Chartres Cathedral could have a pervasive universal significance, it is still valid and informative to look at our artworks as both culturally influenced and influencing. Here, much can be learned by attempting to understand how a work of art was made possible by the unique conditions that surrounded its making, and how the concrete realization

Heidegger's description of art is helpful to us because it provides a map for understanding the elements that make works of art "work." Additionally, his description helps to delineate two distinctly different possible ends for human making—the remarkable and the everyday. However, as you may have noticed, most of the examples cited in the previous section were non-contemporary. This is, in part, because Heidegger believed that the peculiar all-

Relief speaks to the changes in depth or elevation in a given surface. In art, relief is a condition where a surface has been manipulated to create a perceivable depth. Technically, this is a term that pertains to sculptural technique, but may be more generally employed to refer to the depth in a wall, floor, ceiling, etc.

RELIEF

Chartres Cathedral, Chartres, France.

passions—something that someone like Michelangelo could only do indirectly while in the employ of a patron. And then, there are the new avenues that become possible when an artist crosses into uncharted territory—like architect Frank Gehry did for architecture.

Another aspect of our contemporary culture that changes the traditions of art and design is the predominance of capitalism. That is to say, almost everything is now treated as a consumer good, which means that things like shoes, clothes, and tools now *ask to be conspicuous* so that their

Frank Gehry's Disney Concert Hall, Los Angeles, California.

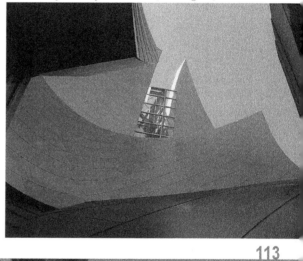

of such works can, in turn, revolutionize what becomes possible in the future. So, for example, Mark Rothko's large color field paintings only become possible in a world after photography has opened new possibilities for painting (beyond representation), where the notion of the spiritual may be freed from a particular religious orientation, and where the definition of the artist allows one to pursue their own

113

A wall with a high degree of relief at the Living Room Theaters, Portland, Oregon.

design might catch the attention of a consumer. Additionally, things that might have been considered utilitarian previously—Shaker furniture, industrial buildings, handwoven goods—now take on a heightened presence as they stand against more mass-produced consumer goods. That is, they move away from their origins as use objects, to become commodities (or art, depending on your perspective). For example, in comparison to a vinyl-clad apartment, a utilitarian vernacular residence becomes a work of art.

Here, some important questions arise about both our notions of art and our notions of utility. We still want, say, our shoes to perform in such a way that we are not conscious of them—we want them to be comfortable. However, there is also a desire to have them "shine" in terms of their noticeability and uniqueness. On the other end of the spectrum, we see buildings, interiors, and landscapes that are "designed," but are so banal and poorly crafted that they become conspicuous in their very ugliness. Here the prod-

Top: apartment, Eugene, Oregon. Bottom: residence, Vals, Switzerland.

ucts of design, formerly inconspicuous in their usefulness, have spread out across a broad spectrum, becoming noticeable in both their beauty and ugliness.

114

The act of adding shade, shadow, and texture to a drawing in order to suggest material, color, and depth.

RENDERING

So, the question is whether one way is better than the other. If we are nostalgic—things aren't made the way they used to be—we say, "Yes, the old way was better." However, we need to be careful; as philosopher Michel Foucault says, "There is in this hatred of the present or the immediate past a dangerous tendency to invoke a completely mythical past."[15] So, it is important to recognize, as we did with art above, that use-things too are products of their times, and attempts to recreate something from the past in the present are usually a recipe for kitsch and superficiality.

However, the modern tendency to make things conspicuous that were traditionally inconspicuous is definitely something to question, because this cultural condition can distract us from the challenges of appropriateness and fit that are so critical to good design. Which is to say, a good design can be well-crafted, perform well, and do its job beautifully without having to be self-important; and this occurs when a designer and their work are responsive to the given circumstances. Further, it is important to remember that beauty does not equal conspicuousness. In other words, something can be beautiful without demanding our at-

Superficial application of historic details: a plastic shutter that is fixed in place (i.e., just for looks) to a fake stone wall on a suburban house.

tention. In fact, this is how one might think of the example of the vernacular structure with the stone roof and why many people find it to be remarkable. It is well-proportioned and finely crafted from substantial

Rendering by fourth-year student Jake Dunn.

both the products of art and design; however, *an artwork* is an exceptional condition, one that arrests us and has no pragmatic function. A work of design, by contrast, must function by connecting to the web of equipment that constantly surrounds us (i.e., a pen needs paper, ink, desks, etc.), and it finds its specific way of shining, in part, by being appropriate—and this does not mean boring or safe—to its given set of circumstances.

In short, our world of advertisements and consumer goods tells us that louder and bolder are better. Art and design must know better and be able to be strategic in finding their own place within. This is a place where one does not have to either rebel against the market—the market is the new patron—or sell out to it. For example, a film by Steven Soderbergh or Wes Anderson can be accepted in the popular market and be financially successful while still retaining its artistic aspirations and results, because their films are not simply built out of explosions and car chases. Both Soderbergh and Anderson actually develop their plots, characters, dialogue, and the look of their films. Like many other contemporary artists and designers, they have remained dedicated to the practice of art, and thus are able to produce work that resonates with both the consumer world and the art world. In this way, design can be both bold and appropriate.

materials—it is beautiful—yet it remains connected to the fabric of its context and thus remains somewhat subtle.

116 So, perhaps we can say this: the products of both art and design may shine, but they shine differently. Here we can see that *art as a practice* (*techne*) remains constant for

A bold urban landscape intervention on the waterfront, Barcelona, Spain.

instruments of design

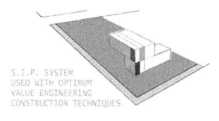

S.I.P. SYSTEM
USED WITH OPTIMUM
VALUE ENGINEERING
CONSTRUCTION TECHNIQUES

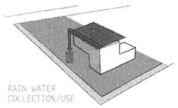

RAIN WATER
COLLECTION/USE

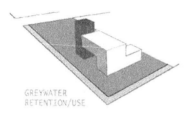

GREYWATER
RETENTION/USE

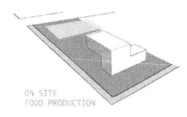

ON SITE
FOOD PRODUCTION

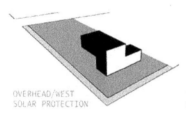

OVERHEAD/WEST
SOLAR PROTECTION

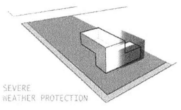

SEVERE
WEATHER PROTECTION

STORMWATER
RUNOFF CLEANSING

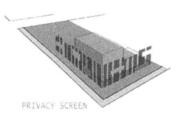

PRIVACY SCREEN

DRAWING

to discover

"It is only by drawing often, drawing everything, drawing incessantly, that one fine day you discover to your surprise that you have rendered something in its true character."[1]

Camille Pissarro

"Studies of a Woman Sleeping," Sir Anthony van Dyck.

Drawing is a fundamental design tool, one that is seen in the very origins of art. And regardless of your discipline, it should be thought of as one of your most important tools for both representing and thinking. However, there are four fallacies about drawing that can interfere with its usefulness and vitality.

First is something that we touched upon earlier in the book, namely that the primary goal of drawing is to represent things literally and accurately. This is only one of many things that drawing might do, and in fact, there are many roles that drawing can play in your work and many types of drawings that can be used to communicate different things. For example, the diagram is a type of drawing that is hugely effective at communicating big ideas or basic strategies in a direct and highly focused manner, and is also extremely helpful when one is processing data. Another type of drawing that is beneficial to the designer is the sketch. The sketch is often effective because of its very ambiguity, in that sketches allow room for one's imagination to make discoveries and see possibilities. Rather than seeking to represent literally, these types of drawing seek the unearthing,

A technique used to suggest continuity or cohesion by way of an element or elements that reappear at intervals throughout a work. This could be in an array, or might be done without contiguity. An example of the latter can be seen in the exhibit design for the U.S. Holocaust Museum. In this project, certain themes, people, and places reappear throughout the experience. Here, memory is being utilized as a means to create continuity. Further, the calling upon of memory is also employed metaphorically as a way to suggest the importance of keeping the memories of the Holocaust alive, so that we never repeat it.

REPETITION

translation, and clarification of ideas that are preliminary, in process, or complicated. Here it is important to remember:

> Recognition of the drawing's power as a medium turns out, unexpectedly to be a recognition of the drawing's distinctness from and unlikeness to the thing that is represented.[2]

A second fallacy about drawing is that drawings are only useful after one becomes highly accomplished at making them. Certainly, there are higher degrees of communication the better one becomes at drawing; however, any mark on paper has the potential to express, suggest, or communicate. For example, imagine a visitor in a foreign country who is unskilled in the native language. This limitation does not mean that they are unable to communicate. Gestures, facial expressions, and short phrases can be surprisingly effective means of expressing oneself. It is the same with drawing: you will be surprised by how well small gestures and partially formed marks can evoke, inspire, and clarify your thoughts.

The third fallacy about drawing is that skill at drawing is an inborn talent. This belief was definitely something I grew up with. There were certain kids in school that everyone thought of as "artists" because they could make drawings that looked like recognizable people and things. The effect of this categorization was that the rest of us just figured that we were not to be artists because we were not born with that talent. Contrary to this belief, drawing is like many other skills—something that can be learned, improved, and mastered though practice. However, like any skill you seek to acquire, it takes dedication and time to improve—"drawing incessantly," as Pissarro said—a fact that reinforces the need to develop habits of excellence.

A fourth fallacy about drawing is the idea that drawing will be irrelevant to those working in a medium that is not directly rooted in drawing. Yet, even if one plans to be a sculptor or to do digital art and design, the basic ideation and communication that occur through drawing are critical to the designer's thinking and an effective design process. The speed and ease of drawing as a means to generate and record ideas is unparalleled. With this in mind, process drawing might be defined as simply *thinking through one's pencil*. This point about

Cemetery, Kyoto, Japan.

principles of design

drawing is fundamental, because if we think about drawing as a tool to communicate ideas, the first people who need to understand these ideas are the designers themselves. In this regard, a drawing might be a completely unintelligible scribble (to outsiders), but could be the very crystallization of an idea for the designer. In this way, drawing works just like the way writing something down can help you remember or make sense of your thoughts. In fact, this kind of transcription will often uncover thoughts you didn't even know you had. Drawing too helps one process visual/physical ideas as well as create a record of these ideas that not only can be referenced later, but perhaps more importantly, can be set side-by-side with other drawings to begin to reveal patterns, relationships, and opportunities—things you cannot see without engaging in this process. Drawing is a powerful tool for all disciplines for this very reason, and should be thought of as, perhaps, the most basic engine of the design process; it brings the ephemeral ideas of the designer into a concrete but malleable form.

COMPOSITION

"When I design buildings, I think of the overall composition, much as the parts of a body would fit together."[3]
Tadao Ando

Composition is the particular arrangement of the different elements in a work, and as a principle it points to the importance of thinking about how the different parts that make up your work speak to one another. A strong composition usually has a senesce of balance, cohesion, and wholeness; taking ownership of a work's composition is the first step toward its refinement and resolution.

Film director Wes Anderson is a good person to look at for tips on composition. I cite his films particularly because they are often thought of more for their peculiar characters and uncanny settings; yet, it is not just that Anderson brings together interesting conceptual or material realities, it is *how* he brings them together. That is to say, Anderson not only understands the importance of thoughtfully composing individual shots, but also has a tremendous talent for

Rhythm in design functions like it does in music, where the rhythm section serves to unite the band and keep it in time. Rhythm in design addresses the fact that a repetition, array, or pattern will also have a certain interval or beat, and as it does in music, rhythm in design helps to unify the work through a kind of spirit that is associated with a particular timing and articulation of the beat. An obvious example would be the different rhythms that are created using columns on building facades and the way that these rhythms create a different spirit for each project.

RHYTHM

"Smoking Scene," William Michael Harnett.

doing so; and the compositional qualities of his films elevate them to the status of art.

Further, Anderson is skillful at with composition not just in terms of composing individual shots but in terms of composing shots across a span of time. Take, for example, the opening sequence to his film *The Royal Tenenbaums,* where he strings together a series of vignettes of the main characters. The way that this sequence works is that each character is shown in

Different column rhythms on buildings in Italy.

principles of design

peculiar settings with clothing and acces-
sories that are indicative of their idiosyn-
crasies; he uses this sequence as a means of
suggesting the ensuing interactions that
will be possible throughout the film as
these strange people cross paths, engage
one another, and share the same spaces.

The example of Wes Anderson obviously
pertains to any filmic art, but it also applies
to digital design in terms of the interdependence between skillfully composed screens
and an overall strategy for the way one
moves through them. It is this interdependence that allows such a time-based experience as a video game or a website to coalesce in one's memory as a single entity.

Such interaction between scene and sequence also applies to design in the built
environment. Here, we are constantly en-
countering moments of transition and moments of focus as we move from place to
place. In this way, composition in the built
environment, like film, is both static and
dynamic; and such an understanding of it is
critical to the coherence of any location and
its relationship to its surroundings.

POPULATING
design

"You can design and create, and build the most
wonderful place in the world. But it takes people to
make the dream a reality."[4]
Walt Disney

Speaking of this dynamic aspect of design in the built environment, time is
often hard to deal with in imagining the
way your project will address and invite activities, interactions, and natural processes.

Entourage is a term that is used to speak
about the representation and use of people,
trees, vehicles, buildings, dogs, birds, and
other things of the world to activate a drawing. However, to merely think about these
things as additions (things to highlight your
design) misses the basic lessons of context
we have talked about throughout the book.
An interior designer, for example, who is
not thinking about how people are using
his space as he designs would seem to be
missing the whole point of design, because
he would be eliminating the temporal realities of the way this place would be inhab-
ited. So, first and foremost, entourage
should be thought of as an instrument that
is used to envision the forces that are at
play in a given design and should be some-

This is a rule of composition that says that if you were to divide your work into thirds
both horizontally and vertically, the most decisive moments should fall upon the lines
and intersections of those divisions. However, because this is art and not science, the
rule of thirds is not an immutable truth, but a suggestion for thinking about composition.
It is a technique that is frequently employed when cropping photos.

RULE OF THIRDS

thing that a designer begins with, not something they add later. That is, if you were designing a doghouse, you would probably want to start with the dog and the area where the doghouse is to be located—a house that does not fit the dog or the site, or does not properly shelter the dog from its local climate, would certainly be a total failure.

In short, entourage should always be used as a means of orienting your design to a particular place and its population. I tell architecture students all the time that if, for example, they are going to draw a street view of their project, they should start with the street view itself and then design their buildings by responding to this view. Such an approach acknowledges the fact that the whole reason for making a building in the first place is because you are trying to add something to, improve, or fit a particular place. If designers think about the elements of entourage as a starting point for understanding a design, rather than finishing ornamentation, then they move away from making interiors, landscapes, buildings, and places that address only their own self-interested creativity. In this way, design becomes beautiful because it is useful and responsive and adds to the places in which it exists.

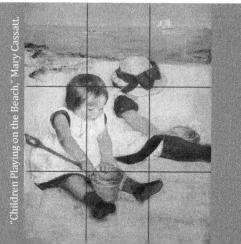

"Children Playing on the Beach," Mary Cassatt.

Entourage in a restaurant design.

often referred to as a design concept. A design concept speaks to one's intention in making certain moves in a creative work, and is an attempt to clarify what is significant about the work. In short, a concept describes the "rules" a design plays by, and this occurs by trying to understand the logic that holds a design together (or could hold it together). Such an understanding begins to illuminate the sorts of design moves that matter within your project and

constructing
CONCEPTS

"There is nothing worse than a sharp image of a fuzzy concept.[5]
Ansel Adams

Part of developing more precise understandings of our design work comes from our ability to describe it. First and foremost, designers must be able to articulate *to themselves* what it is, exactly, that they are doing. This type of description is

Identity as Cube concepts: clockwise from top left, students: Amelia Marek, Aaron Borchardt, Lindsay Eliason, and Rob Cummings.

Scale is a term that can be used to mean the relative size of a work, or can be used to talk about a representational construct. First, as relative size, the term *scale* refers to the proportions of a work and inquires into their fit for the project. It might be used to discuss the size of a canvas—a small canvas is not the proper scale to represent the chaos of the universe—or it could be used to say that the 30-foot height of a ceiling is not in scale with the intimacy of your restaurant design.

In its other application, *scale* refers to the drawing techniques where actual measures are drawn "at scale" in order to make them presentable. It is generally understood that as your scale gets

SCALE

which moves should be excluded from it. For example, in a project where students were asked to translate their personality into cubic form, students had to be able to understand and describe what aspects of themselves were important to the piece and how they could begin to transfer these intentions into material and form. Such conceptual questions help you to develop your ideas, process possibilities, and move a design forward.

One problem students often have with conceptual descriptions is that the concept will often be used as a kind of abstract justification. The concept as abstract justification is frequently experienced in design reviews where students claim their projects to be about some basic one-word or one-sentence generalization, like space, light, movement, flow, hinging, bridging, suspension, openness, nature, etc. These sorts of descriptors are fine beginnings; however, if they also become an end, they are at best un-useful, because they lack the precision we talked about in other parts of the book; and at worst, such limited concepts become no more than an excuse, because they do not contribute to the life of the project—

they define the work but do not intensify its presence.

Part of the reason that people end up with such un-helpful concepts is, simply, that it takes more thought to develop a good description than a bad one; and frequently, just having any description that pertains to your design feels like a relief. However, the difference between an ill-formed concept and a well-formed concept can be the difference between a good project and a great project. For example, at a graduate review a student was explaining how in his design for a soccer facility he had observed that soccer was a game of "continuous movement," and he then went on to substantiate a series of architectural resolutions as being driven by "continuous movement." Yet "continuous movement" is neither good nor bad in itself, *it just is*. And as it was being used, it did not clarify how the place would function or what it would feel like, but merely attempted to rationalize certain formal moves—to give them a reason.

However, if this idea of "continuous movement" had been used as a lens that provided

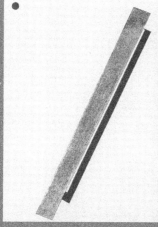

The dot feels even smaller next to the rectangular elements, and conversely the rectangular elements feel even larger next to the dot. Illustration to "Suprematic tale about two squares," El Lissitzky

larger, the level of detail increases, and that the scale of the drawing should correspond to the type of information you are trying to communicate. A site in a landscape might get represented at 1'=1/64", which would make all its parts appropriately small. A building might be drawn at 1'=1/16", an interior room might be 1'= ¼", and a construction detail or industrial design shop drawing might be shown at 1'=1½".

principles of design

a point of view on the project and allowed the student to better process and respond to the complexities of the situation and the realities of human inhabitation and experience, the concept could have become a means to push the project that extra distance it needed to go in order to achieve greatness. In short, problems like this arise when concepts do not grow into the same specificity, subtlety, and force as the inspiration from which they have arisen and the situation into which they are entering— your concept and your project need to evolve together. This is why Deleuze and Guattari claim:

> There are no simple concepts . . . every concept has components and is defined by them. It therefore is a combination. It is a multiplicity, although not every multiplicity is conceptual. There is no concept with only one component.[6]

Here, the importance of rhizomatic thinking returns to help us better understand and utilize design concepts; in fact, good concepts are directly related to the rhizome diagram seen in the process section of this book. The rhizome diagram shows that "*every concept has an irregular contour* defined by the sum of its components."[7] This statement reinforces the idea that, in design, making and thinking are deeply interconnected, and that it is only when the two evolve together that a design can reach maturity. Further, the rhizome diagram shows us that a concept is a set of rules that are subject to revision through their very application—the rules get better understood and refined the more you attempt to apply them. For example, imagine that you are designing a park and you first say to yourself, "I am going to use trees to divide planted areas from areas of human activity." But as you begin to do this, you realize that you had not fully understood the scope of the activities that were to take place on site or all the site conditions. So, when it comes to your attention that a small south-facing bluff might be a nice place for a picnic, you realize that planting trees between the two areas would put your picnic area in the shade. Here your rules get reprocessed to now say, "Trees will be planted to divide the areas of highest human traffic from the most delicate areas of planting; *however, a break in the trees can be used to designate and facilitate special moments* of interplay between these two types of area." In this way, "all concepts are connected to problems without which they would have no meaning and which can themselves only be

Section refers to a type of drawing that is used for slicing something in half, "sectioning" it. A section can be a powerful revealer and communicator of a volume's contents, assembly (how it goes together), and perhaps most importantly, space. If it is done well, a section can be, arguably, the most spatial drawing a designer can employ.

SECTION

isolated or understood as their solution emerges."[8] Thinking rhizomatically does not define a problem so that one can address it instrumentally; rather, one makes things to understand problems, and in this way a concept and solution must necessarily emerge together.

In light of the rhizome diagram, a concept can no longer be seen as a verbal recounting of a causal chain that validates the ends of a project (i.e., the steps you took in a design process neither validate or invalidate your design). Instead, a design concept might be better thought of as a structure that gathers the project around the issues of a particular problem. However, the only manner in which one can truly understand said problem is by responding to what one thinks the problem to be.

METAPHOR
and MIMESIS

"The vampires have always been metaphors for me. They've always been vehicles through which I can express things I have felt very, very deeply."[9]
Anne Rice

principles of design

Section of the Pantheon by Giovanni Battista Piranesi.

Sometimes adding a filter to your thinking can be a useful way to process the things that matter in a design. Metaphors are one kind of filter and might be thought of as a particular type of concept. Strictly speaking, a metaphor is the comparison of one subject or idea with something else that is different in kind yet somehow related. It is the combination of being fundamentally different and in some way parallel that provides a unique perspective on the work in question. Metaphors are useful to designers, because a metaphor can be a means to see a problem in a new light, and as such can stress key issues within the problem. I told a student the other day that her design might be thought of as a shoe that didn't have any laces (the implication being that she needed laces in order to make the design complete). In this way, metaphors in design are a way of seeing a problem with new eyes or framing a way to think about and approach a particular problem. For example, in a project for a theater in an existing building in Amsterdam, the designer said that she imagined the new theater piece as a large piece of furniture that she would insert into the center of the building. This metaphor implied a certain presence of the piece as an object sitting in space—it should feel like a piece of furniture—and its relation to the rest of the building—it should be placed inside the existing building, as opposed to connecting with or altering the shell of the building. One important thing about metaphors—do not ever build the metaphor; otherwise it is no longer a metaphor.

Related to metaphor is another method of comparative inspiration. This method is articulated through the Greek word *mimesis*, which is the root of the word *mimic*. *Mimesis* carries similar connotations to what *mimic* implies—copying—however, it adds another dimension to the simple replication of mimicry through its valuation of the copy as a means instead of an end. In this way, *mimesis* is less of an imitation and more of an initiation of a process of interpretation.

The basic idea of *mimesis* is that a designer begins by finding and imitating an object of physical inspiration. They then proceed through an iterative design process to evolve this initial "mimicry" into a unique entity that specifically fits a design problem. This occurs as the problem requirements are folded into the initial design re-

130

A two-dimensional closed object.

SHAPE

sponse through the process of making a series of variants on the initial theme. The benefit of mimesis is that it provides both an easy entry point—find something that has relevance to your design problem and copy it as directly as you can—as well as a value system that is meant to encourage evolution. In short, *mimesis* escapes the difficulty of trying to envision uniqueness in a vacuum (i.e., not doing what has been done before) by recognizing that what has been done before can be the doorway into a to-tally unique realm; it sets up a process that seeks uniqueness through the connection with, and translation of, a direct, obvious, physical parallel. In the end, a mimetic piece should have little resemblance to the object (or objects) of inspiration, because when properly executed the mimetic process should allow a design to find its own form that is reflective of both the specific usefulness of the inspirational piece and the new purposes that the design is intended for.

Evolution of the Elliptigo.

A composition of shapes: "Non-Objective Composition (Suprematism)," Olga Rozanova.

principles of design

An excellent example of *mimesis* can be seen in the design of a street bike with an elliptical drive called the Elliptigo. Elliptigo was inspired by a guy who loved the mechanics of the elliptical trainers in the gym, but hated being inside. He then worked with a designer to imagine an elliptical trainer that could be ridden outside. It was like the reverse of the evolution of the stationary bike.

DATA

"It is a capital mistake to theorize before one has data."[10]
Arthur Conan Doyle

Data is important to the designer. Its importance ranges from the things a client talks about, to material characteristics

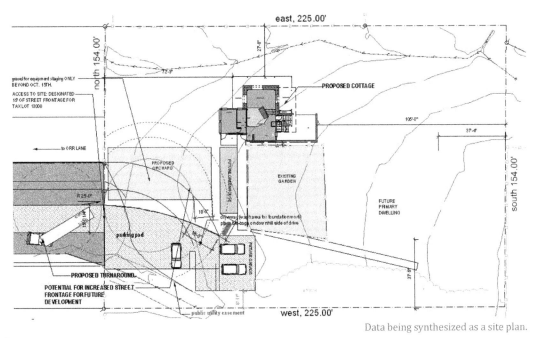

Data being synthesized as a site plan.

A sign is a combination of signifier and signified. That is, a sign is made both of the words and/or graphic (a signifier) and the mental image or message that it evokes (signified). Our world is filled with signs, from billboards to road signs to logos. Art and design can utilize the workings of the sign, either literally in the design and communication of information (graphic design), or as an evocation in a work of art.

and strengths, to the conditions and forces present at a site. However, data is not useful if we just think about it as raw information—there are three processes that all data should undergo to become useful.

First, as Arthur Conan Doyle suggests, data must be collected. This is the process that is most obvious and most utilized. In collection, a landscape architect might go out and map the topography of a site, a digital designer might catalogue a client's requirements for a website, or a sculptor might go talk to a fabricator about the properties of different metals and ways to assemble them. Data collection is the finding, compiling, and arranging of information related to your project.

The next phase of data processing is analysis. Analysis is the act of going through one's collected data and asking *what it all means*. In architecture this might be understanding, for example, that one's collected sun position data indicates a potential problem with heat gain in the building because of the presence of late afternoon summer sun on the site. Analysis is critical, because if you do not understand why your data is important or how it is relevant to your work, it is useless.

Once you collect your data and understand something of its significance, you must synthesize it into your work. Here the landscape architect might need to devise a drainage scheme in relation to her topography data, the digital designer might decide that the requirements of the web project demand a Flash site instead of an HTML one, and the architect might design an exterior screen as a building feature in order to mitigate the heating effects of the afternoon sun.

These different states of data are important to recognize, because too often designers will either overlook data altogether or collect data and simply leave it in its raw state, imagining it to be somehow useful this way. This latter belief is problematic because, first of all, data at the collection stage is to the designer what raw wheat is to the baker—neither is useful to the task at hand. A baker needs the wheat to be transformed into flour; the designer needs information to be transformed into insight. Second, in presenting, say, a diagram of merely collected data, you are asking your client, teacher, or peer to process (analyze and synthesize) the data themselves. This is your job as the designer—to process,

A composition of shapes: "Non-Objective Composition (Suprematism)," Olga Rozanova.

visualize, and present significance, insight, and solutions.

living
HISTORY

"It takes an endless amount of history to make even a little tradition."[11]
Henry James

History is important to the designer because it provides a vast record of human achievement and the potentialities for art and design—both realized and unrealized—across time. Further, the notion of history, as our past, invokes the very temporality of our being. It reminds us that every moment is becoming both a moment future, and a moment past; and as such we are deeply indebted to, and contributors within, this ongoing play of time. Simply, being in time is being human.

Layers of history overlapping at the Louvre, Paris, France.

Here it is important that we do not conceive of time as a series of "nows" that string together the past, present, and future. Instead, our involvements are always characterized by duration.[12] In other words, we do not live in a series of present moments disappearing into the next moment; rather, we live across a time span, where really the "present" does not exist as a discrete moment. The present moment is always an overlapping of past experience and future possibility. That is to say, in a sense, there is no present. Of this condition, Hei-

A sketch is an informal drawing. Often sketches are done under certain limited time frames, and perhaps most importantly, sketches are one of the primary means for connecting thinking and making. That is, in the design process, sketches often amount to thinking visually.

SKETCH

degger has said that existence "*is* what it *was*."[13] In other words, your personal "history" is what allows you to find present situations and future possibilities meaningful and significant in particular ways. This is important to the designer in a variety of ways; however, right now we will focus on how this understanding of time might alter the way we look at history and historical precedents.

History should not be thought of as a storehouse of people and things that have passed from existence and thus have become inert—a collection of precious objects behind glass, as it were. Rather, following the description above, the past is always affecting the present from the point of view of personal experience as well as collective historical experience. And since time is not just a series of discreet nows, that means that daily events and opportunities are not linearly determined: rather, they are the mixing of specific historical potentials becoming future prospects. For instance, being hired to design a professional basketball arena becomes a possibility only because this opportunity has been instantiated by world-historical events, such as Dr. James Naismith's invention of the sport, the

emergence of a public desire to watch this sport, the development of a professional organization that ensures there will be teams to compete against one another in this sport, and, of course, the existence of the architectural profession itself, which has a role in designing arenas for this sport.

Following this line of thought to a more personal scale, the fact that not everyone becomes, or even aspires to become, a designer highlights another important aspect of this living understanding of history; that is, there is an inseparability between the personal aspects of history (your life) and the greater frame of history proper—something in your life led you to design as a profession and history had to evolve in such a way that there became a design profession to aspire to. Such examples illustrate how these two different scales of history are substantially enmeshed and, in fact, cannot exist without the other.

When we begin to think of history in this way, we give ourselves the opportunity to reassess history based on new experiences. Karl Löwith provides an example of this kind of relation to history:

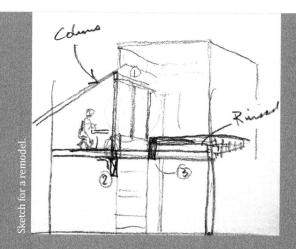

Sketch for a remodel.

principles of design

Christianity, which seemed to Tacitus and Pliny an insignificant Jewish quarrel, conquered the Roman Empire; another quarrel, that of Luther, divided the Christian church. Such unpredictable developments, even when unfolded and established, are not solid facts but realized potentialities, and as such they are liable to become undone again.[14]

Rooftop air conditioning units.

With an ability to reassess history comes the potential for discovering, recovering, or activating possibilities that may not have been taken up at a certain time, but might become relevant again with new information. A good example of this is found in the modern adoption of air as the primary means of heating and cooling buildings. Kiel Moe argues that this "thermodynamically irrational mode of heat transfer" was, at the time, simply one of several possible ways of conditioning buildings, and it became dominant not because of its suitability but because of a mix of "social, economic, marketing, and physiological" factors that obliterated other methods of heating and cooling.[15] Moe goes on to say that as air's efficacy in thermodynamic

transfer is increasingly called into question, there arises a new potential for previously unrealized or dismissed historical methods, like water, to become future realities.[16]

When history is understood as something precious and fixed, it gets stripped of its ability to generate lessons, directions, and meaningful influence. For example, in a second-year design studio project we have done for a bathhouse, it is not uncommon for students to find the Roman baths intriguing. Unfortunately, it is common for this example to be used only merely for its colonnades, vaults, and décor. Taking the next step, a step where history sheds its representational seductions and becomes a spirit or affect permeating the project, is

A three-dimensional volume. Often, being in space implies a sense of being able to "feel" this volume. So although space is ephemeral (immaterial), it is still tangible in the sense that it is real, experienceable, and structured by material things.

SPACE

more difficult and happens less frequently. An example of such a next step might be found in Peter Zumthor's Therme Vals. At Vals, historic potential mixes with local complexities, retaining the basic idea of the Roman *caldarium,* *frigidarium,* and *tepidarium* while allowing these to be reconstituted within a particular time and locale as a kind of quarry or cave made of Valser Quarzite, which is augmented by dramatic lighting and views to the surrounding valley.[17]

These types of transformation are difficult because the next step is always ambiguous, and requires, not representational thinking, but design thinking. Here we might tie this view of history back to the previous discussion of processing data. Rather than either ignoring history as irrelevant to one's work or utilizing it by *collecting* styles and images, one must *analyze* both the objects of history and the events that they have sprung from. The reason for doing this is that analysis generates useful questions about why, say, Michelangelo matters, and why his sculpture is special. Such questions and their ensuing in-

Thermal Baths by Peter Zumthor, Vals, Switzerland.

vestigations become means to rethink our own work and find new avenues for thought and expression. In short, history

Willamette Hall on the campus of the University of Oregon, Eugene, Oregon.

principles of design

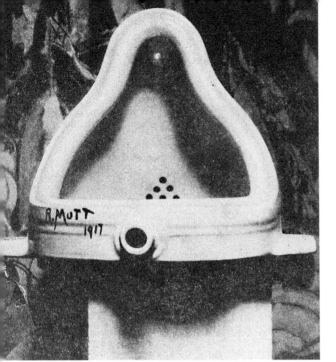

"Fountain," Marcel Duchamp.

OPINION

"Everyday opinions are bland and reductive generalizations."[18]
Claire Colebrook

Art is certainly colored by subjective understandings; however, phrases like "art is in the eye of the beholder" tend to oversell those subjective positions, making it seem like art is just whatever one makes it to be and there is no common ground. Often such beliefs arise because of a lazy intellectual position that is best referred to as opinion. We have to be careful of opinion in art and design, because it can easily undermine our ability to listen, find commonality, and think critically about things.

Here we are talking about a specific definition of opinion: an uninformed, knee-jerk reaction to something that is unfamiliar; a reaction that is falsely built upon an idea that one can just apply their own experience to someone else's perspective without doing any work. That is, if you see Marcel Duchamp's "Fountain" for the first time and you respond by saying you don't

is always relevant to our design work, but in order for it to become most impactful, we need to not just think about what things look like, but how the interrogation of these things and their context changes the way we see the world around us and the work we produce within it.

The use of a series of images to begin to explain the narrative aspects of an idea. A storyboard often is composed of a series of key frames that evoke the whole of the project. That is, what is not represented directly is implied in the space between the things that are represented. Storyboards are important because they allow time to be factored into your design.

STORYBOARD

like it, this response assumes that you and Duchamp are intensely similar (i.e., he is doing variations of things that you already understand), and therefore you do not need to invest any time into understanding the work itself, Duchamp as artist, or the intentions of Dada art. Opinions here destroy curiosity, investigation, and our spirit of discovery, and this destruction leads us to treat rich or complicated experiences simplistically.

This issue with opinion is a critical point, because to be a good artist or designer you must be diligent and inquisitive, trying to learn about things that you do not understand or have never even thought about before. Once you have learned and understood, then you can have a critical discussion; until then, it behooves you to withhold your judgment. We learn much more by entertaining even the most seemingly outrageous ideas and inventions than by deciding ahead of time what kind of person we are, what we like, and what kind of art and design is good (and conversely, what is not). Without curiosity and an ability to suspend disbelief, it becomes impossible to grow as a person, and this shortcoming will leave you with very little to contribute

to any meaningful conversation about art and design.

Opinion of this sort is one of the major obstructions to having a meaningful encounter with design theory as well.

injecting
THEORY

"It should not be forgotten that art is not a science where the latest 'correct' theory declares the old to be false and erases it."[19]
Wassily Kandinsky

Theory comes from the Greek word *theoria*, which means "to see" or "to look at." This basis for theory is important to remember because it reminds us that the goal of theory is to look at and contemplate things in order to make their workings more explicit to us. In other words, effective theory is deeply tied to our practices and our attempts to understand them better. Throughout this book one encounters such use of theory as the making explicit those aspects of our human experience that should be considered as fundamental to our very existence and the designs that emerge from it. In fact, much of this book is

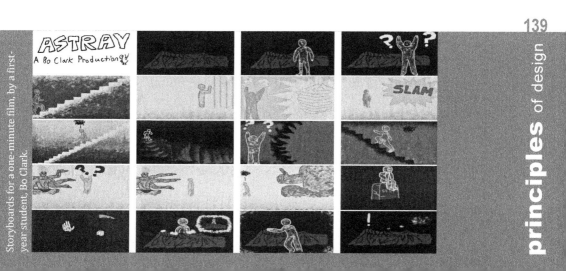

Storyboards for a one-minute film, by a first-year student, Bo Clark.

of the studio, although its language should differ from the household talk of painters and sculptors."[20] This different language can be challenging.

One of the great obstacles to making theory relevant is that the texts that communicate it are generally very difficult reading. Sometimes this is because they are poorly written, but often it is simply because the ideas themselves are complicated. The first thing to bear in mind when reading theory is that it is a different type of endeavor than reading novels, newspapers, magazines, webpages, or even textbooks. Because most of us are used to reading the latter types of texts, our initial encounter with theory will be colored by the density of the text—often it feels like hitting an impenetrable wall of information. However, do not let this first impression discourage you; theory is a different animal than most texts, but like anything else, it gets easier the more practice you get, and its rewards can, at times, be astounding.

Here are a few tips when reading theory:

- First, always begin with the assumption that whatever you are about to

concerned with unpacking the underlying structures of the ways we think, the way experience the world, and the design process itself, in order to make us better designers. On this note art theorist Rudolf Arnheim suggested that "good art theory must smell

Subtractive speaks of a way of making that works by taking material away. An example would be wood or stone carving, where the artist starts with a piece of material, then whittles, carves, and shapes it into the form they desire. Subtractive making can also refer to the sensibilities of a piece and how it feels. That is, there are occasions where, say, a cup or building has the sense of wholeness that goes along with subtractive making, even though it was, in actuality, built up out of many parts. Examples like these are said to have a subtractive form.

SUBTRACTIVE

read is deeply important in some way, even if later it proves not to be. Too often, students will read a difficult text and quickly conclude that it is not useful, interesting, or important, when in fact they have not really understood what was being said; this is where one must be wary of opinion. In short, start every theory reading with an earnest belief in its inherent genius. Certainly, this genius is not always the case, but it will save you the embarrassment of dismissing a text that you have misunderstood, and maybe even lead to a revelation or two.

- It is usually best to read an unfamiliar theory reading once straight through, marking interesting or confusing passages. This technique is opposed to a typical trap of trying to dig out meaning sentence by sentence. Frankly, in many theory readings there will be a host of things you do not understand, but that does not mean that you are not getting something from them. This is why theory must be ruminated—the beauty (and difficulty) with theory is that it is resistant to

simple understandings and explanations, and is resilient in its informational wealth. That is to say, one can read certain articles over and over and find new revelations each time. Theory asks that you live with it and revisit its ideas. You may only get a glimmer the first time you read something, but the glimmer suggests that it is a text you should reexamine from time to time; it will surely yield more insights.

- Think about how the author's ideas relate to things you can relate to in the world. This is an important point, because when theory is seen as a kind of word puzzle—that is, something that does not refer to the world of our experience in any way—then generally it will be misunderstood. Here, as a reader, one is obliged to try to pay attention to the phenomenon that the reading in question describes and attempts to make more explicit.

- Treat every author as if they were doing their very best to communicate a difficult idea without stripping it of its nuance and complexity. Although

Specially cast concrete block, St. Johns Guesthouse, Collegeville, Minnesota.

principles of design

there will always be texts that are more difficult than they need to be, it is much more productive to imagine yourself collaborating with the author to understand something (as opposed to imagining them to be trying to make you feel dumb or willfully writing obscurely). You will find that there are even times where the very peculiarity of an author's delivery is a means for them to get at the difficult truths they are trying to approach.

- We live in a society that is shot through with forums for opinion: most electronic media sources have places for immediate comment by the readers, people write their own blogs, and even the television news can be more opinion than fact. Because of this, many have grown up with the notion that the point of reading others' work is to form an opinion if it. Although opinion has its place, as a pervasive practice it is unhelpful because it obstructs more thoughtful analysis and response. If you find yourself agreeing or disagreeing with the author while reading theory, then you are not reading well. Initial readings of theory are not the place for opinions. Rather, one should always earnestly ask themselves, "What is this author trying to communicate? Why does the author believe this topic to be important? How can I connect the discussion to my own experience and practices?" In short, theory is something that you need to steep in. As the philosopher Friedrich Nietzsche said, it needs to be ruminated, or quite literally—chewed on. Read to understand, not to form an opinion.

- The process of rumination is aided by writing. Much like the design process itself, which is often opened up through the experimentation of making things, writing can dredge understandings out of your brain that you did not even know were there. In fact, I am regularly struck by the number of students who begin a theory reading response by writing how confused they were "but would try to say something anyways," then proceed to communicate a reasonable if not profound

A state of balance characterized by the elements on one side of a composition mirroring the elements on the other. Symmetry is often used as a means of achieving a sense of harmony, order, and balance, and is often seen in classical ordering systems.

One downside to the use of symmetry is that when used as a mere visual or formal device, it can frequently be not very conducive to the activities that are going on within or beyond. This occurs in classical architecture and landscape architecture, where

SYMMETRY

insight about the article in question. Write your way into understanding.

WRITING
to understand

"Everything in life is writable about if you have the outgoing guts to do it, and the imagination to improvise."[21]
Sylvia Plath

A lot of artists and designers do not think about writing as being relevant to them—artists and designers make things. However, writing can be an incredible useful tool for thinking, both for clarifying your thoughts and for generating new ideas. Writing functions like the process of making we have talked about throughout the book, in that it is not just a means of communicating, but first and foremost another form of thinking.

When you are stuck, go write down what you are trying to do, what you are interested in, or even just how frustrated you are on this project. And when you use writing in this way, don't think: just write. That is, don't even lift your pen until you have written at least a full page; even if you have to write, "I don't know why I am writing or what I am writing about," it is important to just keep going, because it is sinking into this flow that will allow the ideas to come out.

"Still Life with Letter," William Michael Harnett.

there are many examples of valuing symmetry in and of itself. Instead of being used for its own sake, it is best employed when it serves the integrity of the whole work. For example, a car design that was bilaterally *asymmetrical* (along its long axis) would probably be quite odd.

principles of design

engaging
PRESENTATION

"When I was 14-years-old, I made this PowerPoint presentation, and I invited my parents into my room and gave them popcorn. It was called 'Project Hollywood 2004' and it worked. I moved to L.A. in January of 2004."[22]
Emma Stone

ning students. Unfortunately, the perception that a review is a kind of defense tends to breed bad presentation habits, and these habits limit the learning that can take place during a review.

In terms of bad habits, most often the notion of "defending" one's work leads to presentation strategies that seek to minimize risk of provocation and maximize the effect of logic to shield the project/student from criticism. Ironically, such strategies very often have the very opposite effect—having uninspired reviewers destroy your logic and point out all the flaws in the project. Here it is important to bear in mind that every project that is put up on the wall is, in effect, an argument, and as such it requires that the "author" develop a clear and effective thesis that illustrates the point of the design and the problem

At the culmination of most projects and sometimes while they are in process, a student will be asked to present their work to a peer, instructor, professional, or community member. This event is called a design review. The review process is often unfamiliar and a bit intimidating for begin-

that the work is addressing. In other words, an effective presentation requires being clear about why one's design is different, special, or unique, which naturally reveals the risks one has taken (or not) in proposing a particular design solution. Instead of building a defense or launching into a sales

Synesthesia is an ability to have sensory data register simultaneously with more than one sense: for example, being able to smell color or hear flavors. A number of artists have been purported to possess this capacity; among them were painter Wassily Kandinsky, composer Olivier Messiaen, and poet Arthur Rimbaud.

SYNESTHESIA

pitch, the presenter should practice orienting the audience to those parts of the project that are remarkable, interesting, and innovative. In doing this, hopefully one is merely highlighting what is already evident in the visual aspects of the work. In short, a verbal presentation should amplify the visuals that are already speaking for themselves.

When being reviewed, there are some things you can do to foster a positive outcome. First, although it is critical to believe in your own work, take pride in your achievements, and show a belief in the efficacy of the proposed solution, it is equally important that you find a disposition or perspective that introduces critical distance between you and your work. In fact, this distance is at the heart of becoming a good designer, because it allows one to develop the ability for self-criticality. Now, this does not mean always second-guessing the things one is doing: rather, this means being able to ask questions and pose alternatives in the spirit of moving the work away from myopic one-dimensionality. The latter is typical of design that has not been properly reflected upon, developed, and refined. This critical distance is extremely

helpful when being reviewed, because it provides a platform from which designers and reviewers may interrogate the work together. Such a platform can change the spirit of a review from one of defense to one of collaboration, with everyone in search of possibilities. Ultimately, this is what all design should be working toward.

Another thing that can really help this investigative quality emerge in reviews is to imagine that you have more time to work on your project. Often, there will be project reviews where one does actually have more time; however, a huge percentage of reviews are also "final." Frequently, when it comes to the final project reviews, students will become much more self-protective of their projects and lose their investigative spirit. Certainly this is understandable, but such inflexibility arises out of a confusion about what the return on a final project should be. In architecture, for example, it would be rare that the final project would be a proposal to actually build something; and even if it was, one would assume that the final critiques would be considered, explored, and synthesized before any actual building occurred. Most of the time, your design projects will only live on paper. This

This work attempts to visually respond to J.S. Bach's "St. Matthew's Passion: "St. Matthew," Randall Teal.

is why it is important to remember that the primary purpose of any scholastic design project is to learn. With this in mind, it becomes much easier to allow a final project to move from being a defense toward becoming a fruitful moment to reflect upon the choices, processes, developments, and refinements one has made, in hopes of discovering greater future effectiveness for one's work.

Now, I cannot say that I speak for all reviewers, but I would wager that more often than not, a reviewer does not want to take a student to task, beat up on their project, or poke holes in their logic. However, if this is all a student offers a reviewer . . . well, then, you can imagine where the review tends to go. There is nothing magic about getting a good review; frankly, it is very basic. The best, most fundamental step toward a good review comes from putting in the hours on your project—you would be surprised to see how often effort equals quality, especially at the beginning levels of design. And even if your design does not end up being brilliant at the end of this effort, your project will still reflect that you have been diligently trying to flesh out your ideas, and that these ideas have become more sophisticated than the ones you started with.

Other tips:

Spend time and effort to make a complete, well-crafted layout. The first impression of a good display goes a long way and usually helps put an audience on your side even before you speak.

20' 6' 6" These are the three distances that you will want to think about your work being viewed from. In other words, you work needs to read, and read differently at 20', 6', and 6". At 20' you want someone to see the whole of the work and have it make an impact. In other words, the work must have a presence from across the room. At 6' one should see a bit of the whole and some of the detail. In short, they should understand the content of your work. 6' is usually the distance that everyone does okay with, because it is close to how we see the work when we work on it; it is also the basic level of detail and information needed on a project. 6" is a difference maker, because it is where we find the details and craft of a project. At 6" your specifics should shine, and finish the impressions that were gleaned from 20' and 6'. Great projects have something to offer at each of these distances.

146

A work of art or design does not always need to be harmonious: it can have tension in it as well. Tension can be an effective means of creating energy in a work. The value of tension is seen throughout the performing arts, from Beethoven's music, to the plays of Shakespeare, all the way through many of our contemporary films, television programs, and music. Tension can create suspense, mystery, and sometimes life in a work.

TENSION

Many times, when rendering, students will get caught in the idea that the work should look materially realistic. At times this can be a reasonable approach. However, most often it is better to think of using color strategically: that is, to use color to direct viewers' attention to key elements within the work and to create continuity in the presentation. Full-spectrum rendering often takes a long time, and also, a wide range of color can often confuse the message of a drawing or presentation.

First-year design presentation, Sami Sumpter.

When speaking, brevity is usually an asset. Too often designers will talk the life right out of their drawings by giving too much background, paying too much attention to superfluous detail, or providing dry justifications of every crack and crevice in a design. Be direct, be clear, and be concise—it is okay to leave questions about your project that reviewers can then ask about. However, be warned that brevity requires knowing precisely what your project is about, knowing your design concept well, knowing what makes it good, and being able to direct an audience to these traits.

Limit the backstory when presenting. Certainly there are key pieces of background that help an audience find sympathy with your piece, but generally what you did a week ago or two months ago while you were working on this is immaterial to the quality of the work on the wall. What does your work propose to do? Show the audience how it does what it does.

Know what the problem is that your design addresses. It can be clarifying to ask yourself, "If I was unable to solve one thing in this design, what would be the one thing, if left unsolved, that would make everything else about the design totally irrelevant?"

Convince the audience that the expressed problem that your design addresses is, in

Stair at University of California, San Diego.

147

principles of design

fact, *the* problem, then show them how your design solves it.

Once the discussion about your project begins, get involved with what you have made (and said) as if you were reviewing someone else's work. This not only makes a review into a design conversation, but also brings your experiences and insights into play as part of the discussion. Remember, it is okay to ask reviewers for advice, direction, and feedback regarding things you do not like about your design, things your design does and does not do well, and the places you had difficulty; such honesty helps us learn.

To have a review where "everything is okay," meaning the reviewers did not have much critical feedback to give you, is not a good review. Such a situation arises when your work is un-evocative. A strong reaction against your work is much better than no reaction at all (assuming this reaction is not a product of an incomplete project). A designer should always aim to create proposals that invite people to engage, discuss, challenge. In other words, a design that is clear and committed and clearly demonstrates the effect of a certain and definite direction allows everyone to better see and consider the question of what constitutes the best response to the given criteria. This is what design is all about.

And remember affect, because it indicates the degree to which art can communicate in ways that are incalculable. For artists and designers, this does not mean that we shouldn't talk about art. Instead, it reframes the way we should talk about art. Instead of using language to justify or explain the work, the artist can use a precise description to bring out more clearly what the work is saying for itself. Bruno Latour says, "If your description needs an explanation, it's not a good description, that's all. Only bad descriptions need an explanation."[23]

Third-year presentation model, Tyler Hash.

ethics of design

technology
WITHOUT
techne

"Humanity is acquiring all the right technology for all the wrong reasons."[1]
R. Buckminster Fuller

As we have talked about throughout the book, the *practice of art* (as *techne*) is critical to the quality of the art and design products that we produce. Further, if *techne* were to lose its nuance and sensitivity, then our relationship to art, design, and making would fundamentally change. Heidegger believed that this transformation was occurring through what he called "modern technological thinking." He used this term as a way of calling attention to the total destruction of the Greek ideal of *techne*, and he was particularly concerned about the impacts this transformation would have on the relationship between human-made things and the natural environment. Unlike the more cooperative relationship that had existed between *techne* and *physis*, modern technological thinking is primarily concerned with the productive efficiencies of technology. That is, modern technological thinking is fixated on developing tools that offer increasing degrees of proficiency

Apartment, Eugene, Oregon.

and ease in processing resources and data; and because of this, it tends to disregard all aspects of nature and society except their potential for being a resource. The art of *techne* is lost to instrumental aspects of modern technology, and the reductive

Our world is filled with textures, and artists over the years have understood the potency of texture. This potency can be seen in the depth of paint on a Van Gogh painting, the crispness of a Donald Judd minimalist piece, or the assembled materials of a Kurt Schwitters collage. Despite the obvious potency of texture, sometimes young artists forget to utilize this power, focusing more on line, form, color, etc.

Designers too suffer from this oversight, often forgetting how important touch is to our experience of the world. In the sensory experience section of the book, we

TEXTURE

thinking of thinking-I drives this shift. Simply put, modern technological thinking is the opposite of *techne*: it is not sensitive to the world around it, and is incapable of co-operation or reciprocation. Instead, it is self-involved and dictatorial; it is the human will toward mastery over all things of the earth.

What this means is that modern technological thinking no longer sees trees, it sees lumber; it no longer sees rivers, it sees irrigation and power; it no longer sees gems and minerals, it sees profits. With such a reductive way of seeing the world around us, human beings ultimately become im-mersed in a sea of meaningless facts, where we become completely beholden to numbers, quantities, and measures, and substitute these for human meaning. Heidegger puts a fine point on this transformation, saying that "nature becomes a gigantic gasoline station, an energy source for modern technology and industry.[2] Prior to such single-mindedness, *techne* had always indicated that our processes and our tools were a way to deepen our relationships within the world; with modern technology, we begin to see the richness of the world transformed to mean merely the financial gains that might be made from processing its products.

Trees versus lumber.

Roof garden, Baton Rouge, Louisiana.

discussed the importance of touch and how our eyes extend our sense of touch, but it bears repeating—whether it is the rough surface of a stone path, the smoothness of a Paperstone kitchen countertop, or the soft leather of an Eames lounger, the effects of texture are reaching us constantly, and it is important that we, as designers, are aware of this and seek ways to utilize texture's power to deepen our work.

principles of design

Further, the single-mindedness, rationalization, and instrumentalizing of modern technological thinking is closely aligned with the educational deficiencies we discussed earlier. This alignment is precisely the reason to spend time discussing art as *techne* (and its decline into modern technological thinking), because *techne* is exactly the thing that artists and designers do well; and it is this skill that stands, according to Heidegger, as a "saving power" in the midst of so much resource depletion—natural and human alike. In other words, the skills that artists and designers possess are critical for mitigating the ill effects of modern technological thinking. The reason artists and designers are critical is because the practices of art and thinking of design are deeply instructive when it comes to those other disciplines and practices that fall prey to the simplicity of more linear and reductive methods of thought and production. However, this "saving power" begins only with understanding the differences between *techne* and technological thinking, and it becomes effective when artists and designers are committed to their work as way of life. Here, art takes on an ethical dimension.

ETHICS
as the path to aesthetics

"In an age of strip malls, sterile government buildings, fast food commercialism, and suburban sameness, we believe that educators and the profession should become more effective advocates for beauty in the structures that touch so permanently the lives of everyone in society."[3]

Earnest Boyer and Lee Mitgang

Often times, the question of ethics in the context of design gets limited to professional ethics. Professional ethics tend to deal with such things as life safety, the law, billing, and business practices. All of this is important; however, these topics sometimes tend to leave a more fundamental notion of ethics out of the design discussion. That is, the real challenge for designers is not to make brilliant designs; rather, it is to understand that the most brilliant designs seek to improve the world in some way. So, the ethics we are here concerned with has to do with this challenge, which is to say an ethical designer is always looking to understand more, do better, and push their work further because they want their work to positively affect peoples' lives.

In music, theme and variation is a standard composing technique where altered forms of the original theme collect to become the work itself. Designers can use this strategy as well. As in the musical example, the designer would develop a main theme and then strategically alter it throughout the course of the work, perhaps to fit other needs, functions, or conditions. This is a good way to think of any design that is composed of several parts, because the theme establishes an identity and then, by varying that theme, the designer ensures there will be continuity among the parts while still being able to address the sometimes conflicting requirements of a design.

THEME & VARIATION

The word *ethics* derives from the Greek *ethos*. The term *ethos* originally referred to one's "accustomed place." This is interesting because it suggests ethics is something that should be as basic and familiar to us as our own home. Following this fundamental quality of *ethos*, an ethical designer is one that does not treat design as a mere pastime, a job, or a way to pay the bills. Instead, they think of design as something that we, as designers, live in and must live with; it defines us. Without this attitude, if one just does design to get by, there necessarily ensues an inattention to details, a

Scotlandville, Louisiana.

lack of follow-through, and a general lack of seriousness. In fact, more than anything else, it is this drive to always do better, learn more, and make your work more precise that leads to the most appropriate, expressive, nurturing, shocking, beautiful results. The point here is that because design affects so many people in every aspect of life, to merely dabble in it is flat-out irresponsible; and it is the aforementioned re-

lentlessness that differentiates the ethical designer—the good designer—from the mere dabbler.

This subject is important because, unfortunately, our recent history is awash in a deluge of bad design. From inhuman social housing projects, to poorly made furniture, to communities dominated by cars, to landscapes inappropriately transplanted from

Parking garage, Lyon, France.

principles of design

Watering lawns (and sidewalks) in Palm Springs, California—a place that averages 5.8" of rain per year.

temperate climates into deserts, almost everywhere one looks there is overwhelming evidence of bad design. And, unfortunately, examples like these are not just unpleasant to look at—they also affect the well-being of individual people, communities, and the environment. Now, certainly, some of these bad situations occur simply because life is imperfect and there are no guarantees about how a design will harmonize with the passage of time. However, what we want to avoid is making design choices purely based on aesthetics, functionality, or profit. With these types of missteps in mind, this book attempts to provide the soil to cultivate a balanced process, a full way of

A threshold is a physical element that is usually found in space. It designates the passage from one distinct condition to another: the city to home; the profane to the sacred; cacophony to silence; the rural to the urban. The well-designed threshold can accentuate the experience of crossing over from one condition into another.

THRESHOLD

thinking, and precision in the work that is done—not just to prevent bad design, but also to sow the seeds of good design, which can bring productivity, well-being, and even joy to those who encounter, use, and live it.

the *INTRINSIC*
value of design

"There is something within us that can always find reasons to do what is easy rather than what is right."[4]
Sufi parable

One of my former professors once said that when architecture becomes about making money, it is no longer about architecture. At first this statement is confusing, because it seems to suggest that one should not aim to make a living by doing architecture; or that if one does make a living, they certainly shouldn't make a *good* living. However, my professor intended something a little different than this, and what he intended can be expanded to include the practices of art and design more generally. Having an ethical foundation for your work simply means that you see your responsibility to the world you are designing for analogously to the way you would see your commitment to friends, family, colleagues, and pets. If one's design work shifts from being some-

"An Old Woman Spinning," Nicolaes Maes.

how important in and of itself to something where there is no basis for judging between good and bad work, acceptable or unacceptable options, appropriate or inappropriate projects, one enters a place where the only measure for the worthiness of design is financial gain; here, everything becomes negotiable for the right price, and consequently everything, in turn, loses its intrinsic value. In other words, when

157

Separate adult and child thresholds for passage into the "Imaginarium," Vienna, Austria.

principles of design

priceless things are allowed to be priced and traded as such, their anchoring significance, meaning, and fundamental worth are lost. This is the danger of capitalism. Fredric Jameson points to the dangerous position for art and design within capitalism when he observes, "What has happened is that aesthetic production today has become into commodity production generally."[5] In other words, capitalism has commandeered art and design so that it might sell more consumer products.

This is something we must be cognizant of, but not to the degree that we turn our backs on the market altogether. That is, the message of not making your work become about the money *does not mean* that one should not make money doing art and design. Instead, it means that money must never be the primary motivating factor for the work, because as soon as it becomes this, design gets shaped primarily by market forces; and market forces always reward the most widely accepted, most efficient, and most profitable. In short, money can always be used to justify just about any kind of design choice—if it is profitable— and can cause one to pander to the purchasing populace, thus losing sight of what really matters in their work.

As a counterpoint to a world that is driven primarily by profits, let us again consider the design and building of the medieval cathedrals. In the great cathedral projects, we see endeavors that were considered a worthy expenditure of funds and efforts because they helped to bolster and unify a community around a common good. In order to realize such momentous cultural artifacts, masons and artists often spent many years working on these projects with limited financial reward; and with these buildings sometimes taking a hundred years to complete, often their builders and designers did not even witness the completion of their labors. This noble nature of the great cathedral projects and the way that they exemplified, for many, art and design at its best and most collaborative is one of the reasons they became the exemplar for the great modern design school, the Bauhaus. The school's founder, Walter Gropius, said in his inaugural address:

Together let us desire, conceive, and create the new structure of the future, which will embrace architecture and sculpture and painting in one unity and which will one day rise toward heaven from the hands of a million workers like the crystal symbol of a new faith.[6]

A small quick sketch that is meant to communicate the very basics of an idea. A thumbnail is often utilized in preliminary phases of a design or in making an artwork in order to visually process what is being proposed.

THUMBNAIL

In other words, the pioneers of the Bauhaus had dreams of a new design collaborative—the modern cathedral. This was a noble goal. Unfortunately, the times of the cathedral were unique, so even metaphorically arriving at a new cathedral as a "crystal symbol of a new faith" would have been virtually impossible. However, this effort is still instructive, as it shows us how to be aspirational and points us toward trying to achieve the highest goals in art and design. Additionally, the Bauhaus masters demonstrated an excellent vision of how history might be revisited, not for its styles, but for its processes; and, in turn, how it could be revised by applying proper attitudes and techniques appropriate to one's own time. In this way, we see a notion of history that is not merely a repository of people, things, and events that have passed, but instead is a vital part of our present and a living source for our future.

Further, this view of history represents, perhaps, the most important attitude/skill for a designer to develop—curiosity. Herein lies one of the hidden challenges in a basic design course—*and it is so important*—for students to invest in their own passions for knowledge and learning. Studio art is an instructive example in this regard, because studio artists have to, almost necessarily, operate from this disposition: most of the time no one is asking for their art, and no one is paying them for the amount of art they produce. They do this work, first and foremost, because they care about it.

Finally, when we do get paid for our work, it is important to remember how we got to that place. Otherwise, it is easy for a profit-based mindset to take over and crush the real spirit of your creativity. Take, for example, former rock star Peter Frampton. At his best, he was filling stadiums with people that wanted to hear his music.

The Bauhaus, Dessau, Germany.

Captured pechenegs costume design for the opera "Rogneda," Mikhail Vrubel.

Unfortunately, when this occurred he froze up, asking himself, "What do they want from me now!?" This question shifted his songwriting from a personal process into a process of approval. What ensued was a precipitous fall from the spotlight.

Ultimately, the way one remains an artist is by pursuing the questions and passions of their work unfalteringly. Most artists who do not have this drive will quit doing art and will therefore cease to be artists. Unfortunately for the world at large, design is different, because it is not so personally motivated. It is also a service, a job, a profession, and can therefore very easily become *just* a job. And as the evidence around us suggests, there are many people making money doing design work who do not possess enough dedication, drive, or perhaps love of what they are doing to do it well. It is exactly these motivations that directly connect with questions of quality, the effect their work has on other people, and the impact it has on the environment. As long as design simply equals cash at the end of the day, there will be plenty of practitioners. True designers are artists in that they will continue to do what they do even if it must be supported by other (financial) means

than the work itself. For example, architect Thom Mayne sold paintings and illustrations of his work until he got some small houses and remodels to do; he kept at it and now his firm Morphosis does some of the largest, most prestigious projects in the world.

Unfortunately, we live in an economic system that supports the idea of design as simply a job. And, for better or worse, if someone is willing to pay, just about anything can be created. There are some limitations and controls, like zoning laws in the built environment disciplines, that offer some regulation and vetting. But the ugly side of freedom is the fact that our consumerist culture and its mechanisms offer the perfect engine for producing tons and tons of junk, which, of course, is why designers must take on the challenging ethical questions of design.

In some ways this is extremely hard with the systems we have in place. However, in other ways it is extremely easy—young designers just need to find and foster the things they care about, the things beyond fame and money that motivate their desire to become designers. It also demands that

Topography articulates the relief of the earth's surface. That is, topography delineates the different elevations of a particular place as well as the rate of change between elevations. Topography is like the earth's fingerprint, and as such it reminds us that every place is already unique—the job of the designer is to augment this condition, not treat it as a blank slate.

TOPOGRAPHY

Morphosis' Wayne Morse Federal Courthouse, Eugene, Oregon.

one consider seriously the type of society one wants to live within and imagine what role one might play, as a designer, in moving in such a direction. Ultimately, I think what my professor meant when he said, "When architecture becomes about the money it is no longer about architecture," was that if you are in solely in design for the money, you should do everyone a favor and get out, because such motivation is shallow and short-lived. There is too much work and worry that goes along with being an ethical designer to merely do it for profits, and in the end, design motivated by money will always find its final revisions driven by profits and therefore not concerned enough with the human impacts it makes.

Certainly, we all need to make a living, and in many cases we can make a good living as designers. But doing this well begins by recognizing that there have to be things in

Brindle Canyon, Texas topography.

principles of design

life (and design) that cannot be given monetary value (or at least be compromised for a cash payoff); otherwise, we will find ourselves living in a world devoid of meaning, significance, and human connection. In short, if we do not frame design as an ethical undertaking, we will ultimately design our way into a world that is no longer worth living in.

cal engagement with our world, then we not only reveal the true power of art, but also, through such practices, outline a course for its continued relevance—or better, its necessity.

In these terms, to be an artist means to be attentive, to be curious, and to be capable of being moved by events. It also means developing skills sets particular to specific

the
SAVING POWER
of art

"What we are getting is not the demise of art, but a transformation of the function of art. Art today is a new kind of instrument for modifying consciousness and organizing new modes of sensibility."[7]
Susan Sontag

If we think, as Aristotle suggested, of art more broadly as a particularly thoughtful way of doing things, we can then leave more limited definitions of art behind. That is, if art is merely the pursuit and creation of beautiful things, one might then argue that art holds a place of limited worth for us, because with such a narrow definition, much of art becomes inaccessible in terms of both intellect and finances to most people; however, if art is instead thought of first and foremost as the basis for an ethi-

"Landscape with Peacocks," Paul Gauguin.

A condition where light is transmitted through a material. Buildings obviously utilize this in the form of windows, but transparency can also play out in painting, sculpture, and photography, and is much more easily employed in representational techniques than it used to be because of digital tools such as Photoshop. Transparency can be used very effectively to highlight items without obscuring them, and is an excellent technique in the making of diagrams.

TRANSPARENCY

pursuits. Here, being an artist does not just mean being free-spirited or creative in some vague way: rather, it means mastering the ways of seeing and doing that better allow one to engage and enhance the world in which they live.

Of course, as we discussed throughout the book, this requires an undying commitment to both a rigorous practice and the products that come out of it. And the requisite passion for the work means that although others might not fully understand,

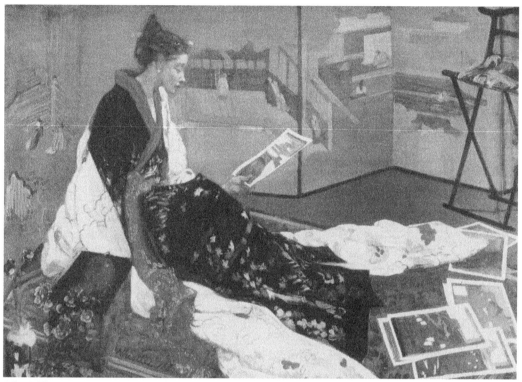

"The Golden Screen," James Abbott McNeil Whistler.

"Pierrot Lunaire," Paul Klee.

principles of design

"Le Moulin de la Galette," Auguste Renoir.

you will do what you need to do in order to feel fulfilled. For example, architect Frank Gehry once gave up a lucrative practice doing work that he found unfulfilling, so that he might be free to pursue design that he really cared about; painter Paul Gauguin left his wife and children for his work; and painter Mark Rothko returned the largest commission of his life when he was unable to reconcile his values with the commis-

Value is the relative state of dark to light in a given work. Value directly relates to contrast. A combination of high and low value (black on white) would be high-contrast, and a combination of like values (say, light grey on white) is low-contrast. Often the reason that a drawing or photo will not read well is because it lacks contrast. Further, interior spaces that have a bad sense of light (think Walmart) are also adversely affected by strategies of low contrast.

VALUE

"Seine Quays," Paul Cézanne.

sion. In short, many artists have been faced with the question of doing what appears to be logical versus what they know they need to do—the ethical question. Many decisions will not be as dramatic as these, but such conundrums are emblematic of the life of an artist.

Although an artist will develop concrete skills and abilities over the course of her education, it may in fact be the intangible skills that prove to be the most valuable. Facility with emotion, intuition, and engaging nonlinear systems can make seemingly mundane tasks artistic. That is, when we

"Basket of Flowers," Jan van Huysum.

A radical acknowledgment of the power of value in creating contrast can be seen in a technique developed during the Italian Renaissance called chiaroscuro. Chiaroscuro sought to utilize the sense of drama and dynamics that could be gained by using a high-contrast strategy in a work. The painter Caravaggio was one of the masters of this technique.

principles of design

approach things like drawing, studying, politics, medicine, accounting, cleaning, designing a house, talking with friends, or raising a family with passion, precision, focus, strong instincts, and a capacity for indeterminacy, our other skills become the most effective and we become the most human.

"At the End of the Day," Jules Breton.

Context of Design

1. Friedrich Nietzsche, *Thus Spake Zarathustra: A Book for All and None*, trans. R. J. Hollingdale (New York: Viking, 1961), 49; Friedrich Nietzsche, *Thus Spake Zarathustra: A Book for All and None*, trans. Thomas Wayne (New York: Algora Publishing, 2003).
2. Mentioned in a presentation to second-year architecture students at the University of Oregon, 2004.
3. "Anthropology under Attack," *Social Science Space*, last modified October 17, 2011, http://www.socialsciencespace.com/2011/10/anthropology-under-attack/.
4. Lyrics from "Beautiful Boy (Darling Boy)," *Double Fantasy*, 1980, Geffen Records.
5. Friedrich Nietzsche, "On Truth and Lying in an Extra-Moral Sense," in *Continental Aesthetics Reader*, ed. Clive Cazeaux (New York: Routledge, 2000), 57.
6. "Collected Quotes from Albert Einstein," accessed June 13, 2012, http://rescomp.stanford.edu/~cheshire/EinsteinQuotes.html.
7. Martin Heidegger, *What Is Called Thinking?*, trans. J. Glenn Gray (New York: Harper & Row, 1968), 21.
8. Herman Melville, *Moby-Dick or, The Whale* (New York: The Modern Library, 2000), 385.
9. Ernest Boyer and Lee Mitgang, *Building Community: A New Future for Architecture Education and Practice: A Special Report* (Princeton: Carnegie Foundation for the Advancement of Teaching, 1996), 77.
10. Ibid., 141.
11. Zicheng Hong, Robert Aitken, and D. W. Y. Kwok, *Vegetable Roots Discourse: Wisdom from Ming China on Life and Living: Caigentan* (Berkeley, CA: Shoemaker & Hoard, 2006), 38.
12. Aldous Huxley, *The Doors of Perception, and Heaven and Hell* (New York: Harper & Row, 1954), 22.
13. Henri Bergson, *Creative Evolution* (New York: Random House, 1944), 34.
14. Descartes, 1986, 16.
15. Ibid., 18.
16. Carol Poster, "Protagoras," *Internet Encyclopedia of Philosophy*, accessed June 13, 2012, http://www.iep.utm.edu/protagor/.
17. Aristotle, *Nicomachean Ethics* (Newburyport, MA: Focus Publishing, 2002), 35.
18. Heidegger, *What Is Called Thinking?*, 8.
19. Ibid., 15.
20. Eknath Easwaran, ed., *The Upanishads* (Tomales, CA: Nilgiri Press, 1987), 144.
21. Actual quote: "The river where you set your foot just now is gone—those waters giving way to this, now this" (Heraclitus, 2003, 27).
22. Alvar Aalto, "Alvar Aalto Speaks," *Virtual Finland*, accessed November 15, 2008, http://virtual.finland.fi/netcomm/news/showarticle.asp?intNWSAID=26191.

Processes of Design

1. Aristotle, *Nicomachean Ethics*, 4.
2. Gilles Deleuze, *Bergsonism*, trans. Hugh Tomlinson and Barbara Habberjam (New York: Zone Books, 1991), 15.
3. Manuel DeLanda, *A New Philosophy of Society: Assemblage Theory and Social Complexity* (New York: Continuum, 2006).

4. "The Quotations Page," accessed June 10, 2012, http://www.quotationspage.com/quote/27038.html.

5. Jim Jarmusch, "Q and A," *Down by Law* (The Criterion Collection, 1986), DVD.

6. Aristotle, *Nicomachean Ethics*, 11.

7. Fredric Lieberman, "Zen Buddhism and Its Relationship to Elements of Eastern and Western Arts," accessed July 11, 2012, http://arts.ucsc.edu/faculty/lieberman/zen.html.

8. Quoted in Hannah Higgins, *The Grid Book* (Cambridge: The MIT Press, 2009), 31.

9. Martin Heidegger, *The Essence of Truth: On Plato's Cave Allegory and Theaetetus*, trans. Ted Sadler (London and New York: Continuum, 2002), 203.

10. "The Painter's Keys," accessed July 11, 2012, http://quote.robertgenn.com/getquotes.php?catid=266&numcats=361.

11. Alvar Aalto, "Abstract Art and Architecture," in *Synopsis; Painting, Architecture, Sculpture* (Basel: Birkhauser Verlag, 1970), 18.

12. "Eliel Saarinen Quotes," *Thinkexist.com,* accessed June 10, 2012, http://thinkexist.com/quotation/always_design_a_thing_by_considering_it_in_its/204270.html.

13. Gilles Deleuze and Felix Guattari, *A Thousand Plateaus: Capitalism & Schizophrenia* (Minneapolis: University of Minnesota Press, 1987), 6–7.

14. Martin Heidegger, "The Origin of the Work of Art," in *Poetry, Language, Thought* (New York: Harper & Row, 1971), 39.

15. Georgia O'Keeffe, "A Second Outline in Portraiture," quoted in Gail R. Scott, *Marsden Hartley* (New York: Abbeville Publishers, Cross River Press, 1988), 167. (Great inspirational woman master artist Georgia O'Keeffe; her quotations about life and creating modern "abstract" landscape painting art; American Modernism: http://www.quotes-famous-artists.org/georgia-okeeffe-45-quotes.)

16. Heidegger, *What Is Called Thinking?*, 46.

17. Martin Heidegger, *Being and Time*, trans. John Macquarrie and Edward Robinson, 7th ed. (San Francisco: Harper and Row, 1962), 405.

18. Deleuze and Guattari, *A Thousand Plateaus*, 493.

19. Heidegger, *What Is Called Thinking?*, 170.

20. Daisetz T. Suzuki, *Zen and Japanese Culture* (Princeton, NJ: Princeton University Press, 1970), 219.

21. Gilles Deleuze and Felix Guattari, *What Is Philosophy?*, trans. Janis Tomlinson and Graham Burchell (New York: Columbia University Press, 1996), 175. My emphasis.

22. Ibid., 173.

23. Heidegger, *What Is Called Thinking?*, 16.

24. Martin Heidegger, *An Introduction to Metaphysics*, trans. Ralph Manheim (New Haven and London: Yale University Press, 1959), 14.

25. Martin Heidegger, *The Question Concerning Technology and Other Essays*, trans. William Lovitt (New York: Harper & Row, 1977).

26. Shunryu Suzuki, *Zen Mind, Beginner's Mind* (New York and Tokyo: Weatherhill, 1970), 106.

27. Søren Kierkegaard, *Fear and Trembling & The Sickness Unto Death*, trans. Walter Lowrie (Garden City, NY: Doubleday Anchor Books, 1954), 59.

28. Ibid., 57–64.

ENDNOTES

29. Alberto Pérez-Gómez and Louise Pelletier, *Architectural Representation and the Perspective Hinge* (Cambridge: MIT Press, 1997), 7.
30. Maurice Merleau-Ponty, *The World of Perception* (New York: Routledge, 2002), 94.
31. Vittorio Gregotti, *Inside Architecture* (Cambridge: The MIT Press, 1996), 48.
32. DeLanda, *A New Philosophy of Society,* 31.
33. Henri Bergson, "Introduction to Metaphysics," in *The Creative Mind* (New York: The Philosophical Library, 1946), 58.
34. Deleuze, *Bergsonism*, 15.

Products of Design

1. Jack Flam, *Matisse on Art* (Berkeley & Los Angeles: University of California Press, 1995), 66–67.
2. Claire Colebrook, *Gilles Deleuze* (New York: Routledge, 2002), 24–25.
3. Juhani Pallasmaa, *The Eyes of the Skin: Architecture and the Senses* (Hoboken, NJ: John Wiley & Sons, 1996), 29–30.
4. Allen Ginsberg, "America," http://www.writing.upenn.edu/~afilreis/88/america.html.
5. Martin Heidegger, *History of the Concept of Time: Prolegomena,* trans. Theodore Kisiel (Bloomington: Indiana University Press, 1985), 188.
6. Edward Casey, *Remembering: A Phenomenological Study* (Bloomington: Indiana University Press, 1987), 206.
7. "Ben Shahn Art Quotes," *The Painter's Keys*, accessed June 13, 2012, http://quote.robertgenn.com/auth_search.php?authid=82.
8. Emily Dickinson, "Tell All the Truth but Tell It Slant," accessed June 13, 2012, http://hellopoetry.com/poem/tell-all-the-truth-but-tell-it-slant/.
9. Heidegger, "The Origin of the Work of Art," 45–46.
10. Melville, *Moby-Dick*, 267.
11. Dan Brown, *Angels & Demons* (New York: Atria Books, 2003), 305.
12. Ludwig Mies van der Rohe, "On Restraint in Design," *New York Herald Tribune*, June 28, 1959.
13. Ken Burns, *Jazz* (USA: Warner Home Video, 2000).
14. "William Morris," *Interior Design Quotes,* accessed June 13, 2012, http://www.interiordesignquotes.com/william-morris.html.
15. Michel Foucault, "Space, Knowledge, and Power," in *Architecture Theory Since 1968*, ed. K. Michael Hays (Cambridge, MA: The MIT Press, 1998), 435.

Instruments of Design

1. John Rewald and Camille Pissarro, *Camille Pissarro* (New York: H. N. Abrams, 1963).
2. Robin Evans, "Translations from Drawing to Building," in *Translations from Drawing to Building and Other Essays* (Cambridge: MIT Press, 1997), 154.
3. Tadao Ando, "Interview from Architectural Record," from *Architectural Record*, May 2002, accessed April 27, 2012, http://www.coldbacon.com/art/tadaoando-interview.html.
4. "Design Quotes of the Day," *Bizcommunity.com*, accessed June 13, 2012, http://www.bizcommunity.com/Quotes/196/13.html.

5. "Ansel Adams," *PhotoQuotes.com*, accessed June 13, 2012, http://www.photoquotes.com/showquotes.aspx?id=10.

6. Deleuze and Guattari, *What Is Philosophy?*, 15.

7. Ibid., 15–16. (my italics)

8. Ibid., 16.

9. "Anne Rice Quotes," *BrainyQuote*, accessed June 13, 2012, http://www.brainyquote.com/quotes/quotes/a/annerice339252.html.

10. Arthur Conan Doyle and Kyle Freeman, *The Complete Sherlock Holmes* (New York: Barnes and Noble Classics, 2003), 189.

11. Henry James, *The American Scene* (New York: Penguin, 1994), 82.

12. Martin Heidegger, *The Basic Problems of Phenomenology* (Bloomington: Indiana University Press, 1982), 263–64.

13. Ibid., 265.

14. Karl Löwith, *Meaning in History* (Chicago: University of Chicago Press, 1949), 198.

15. Kiel Moe, *Thermally Active Surfaces in Architecture* (New York: Princeton Architectural Press, 2010), 42.

16. Ibid., 52.

17. Sigrid Hauser and Peter Zumthor, *Peter Zumthor Therme Vals* (Zurich: Verlag Scheidegger and Spiess, 2007).

18. Claire Colebrook, *Gilles Deleuze* (Taylor & Francis, 2002), Kindle edition, 16.

19. Wassily Kandinsky, Kenneth Clement Lindsay, and Peter Vergo, *Kandinsky: Complete Writings on Art* (Boston: G.K. Hall, 1982), 471.

20 Rudolf Arnheim, *Art and Visual Perception: A Psychology of the Creative Eye* (Berkeley: University of California Press, 1954), 4.

21. Sylvia Plath and Karen V. Kukil, *The Unabridged Journals of Sylvia Plath, 1950–1962* (New York: Anchor Books, 2000), 554.

22. Jillian Gordon, "Emma Stone: Coolest Chick We Know." *Saturday Night Magazine*, accessed April 26, 2012, http://www.snmag.com/INTERVIEWS/Celebrity-Interviews/Emma-Stone-Coolest-Chick-We-Know/Print.html.

23. Bruno Latour, *Reassembling the Social: An Introduction to Actor-Network-Theory*, Kindle edition, 147.

Ethics of Design

1. "Richard Buckminster Fuller Quotes," *SearchQuotes*, accessed June 13, 2012, http://www.searchquotes.com/quotation/Humanity_is_acquiring_all_the_right_technology_for_all_the_wrong_reasons./31364/.

2. Martin Heidegger, *Discourse on Thinking*, trans. John M. Anderson and E. Hans Freund (New York: Harper & Row, 1966), 50.

3. Ernest Boyer and Lee Mitgang, *Building Community: A New Future for Architecture Education and Practice: A Special Report*, 37.

4. Robert Frager, *Heart, Self & Soul: The Sufi Psychology of Growth, Balance, and Harmony* (Wheaton, IL: Quest Books, 1999).

5. Fredric Jameson, "Postmodernism or The Cultural Logic of Late Capitalism," accessed July 11, 2012, http://www.marxists.org/reference/subject/philosophy/works/us/jameson.htm.

6. Ulrich Conrads, *Programs and Manifestoes on 20th Century Architecture* (Cambridge, MA: MIT Press, 1970), 49.

7. Susan Sontag as quoted in Calvin Tomkins, *Off the Wall: A Portrait of Robert Rauschenberg* (New York: Picador), 230.

Context of Design

Page 4: "L'Hôpital Saint-Paul à Saint-Rémy," Vincent Van Gogh: Image courtesy of Corel. Page 7: The Garden of Earthly Delights," Hieronymus Bosch: Public domain, http://www.wikipaintings.org/en/hieronymus-bosch/the-garden-of-earthly-delights-1515-4; Moby: music, too, affects us: Image © vilena makarica, 2012. Used under license from Shutterstock, Inc. Page 11: "Courtyard of Innsbruck Castle," Albrecht Dürer: Image courtesy of Corel. Page 13: Axis: Palace-de-Versailles, France: Image © parkisland, 2012. Used under license from Shutterstock, Inc. Page 17: "The Home Lesson," Albert Anker: Image courtesy of Corel; "Girl with a Broom," Rembrandt van Rijn: Image courtesy of Corel. Page 18: "Aristotle Contemplating the Bust of Homer," Rembrandt van Rijn: Image courtesy of Corel. Page 19: Teamwork: a visual cliché: Image © Andresr, 2012. Used under license from Shutterstock, Inc. Page 24: "Garden Restaurant," August Macke: Public domain, http://www.wikipaintings.org/en/august-macke/garden-restaurant. Pages 26–27: Hampton Court Palace, London, England: Image © Rachelle Burnside, 2012. Used under license from Shutterstock, Inc.

Processes of Design

Page 32: "The Creation," Michelangelo Buonarroti: Image courtesy of Corel. Page 37: Matt Wilkenson, Gold Coast, Australia: Image © Markus Gebauer, 2012. Used under license from Shutterstock, Inc.; "Gooyer Windmill Amsterdam," Claude Monet: Image courtesy of Corel. Page 40: Match between BVB Dortmund and VfB Stuttgart: Image © KENCKOphotography, 2012. Used under license from Shutterstock, Inc. Page 41: Improvisation: Maceo Parker: Image © Sergei Bachlakov, 2012. Used under license from Shutterstock, Inc. Page 42: Rhizome: swarming honeybees. Image © Steven Russell Smith Photos, 2012. Used under license from Shutterstock, Inc. Page 43: "Place de l'Europe on a Rainy Day," Gustave Caillebotte (top). "Yoshida," Ando Hiroshige (bottom): Images courtesy of Corel. Page 44: A rhizomatic system: Bats seeking food at night: Image © Sura Nualpradid, 2012. Used under license from Shutterstock, Inc. Page 47: "Okabe," Ando Hiroshige: Image courtesy of Corel. Page 48: Landscape by Paul Cézanne: Image courtesy of Corel. Page 50: "Hakone," Ando Hiroshige: Image courtesy of Corel. Page 53: "Sunflowers," Vincent Van Gogh: Image courtesy of Corel. Page 54: Beer making in the Unyamwezi region, Tanzania: Image © Antonio Abrignani, 2012. Used under license from Shutterstock, Inc. Page 55: HMS Victory old illustration, Nelson's flagship at the Battle of Trafalgar: Image © Antonio Abrignani, 2012. Used under license from Shutterstock, Inc.; City map of the unknown city: Image © forest badger, 2012. Used under license from Shutterstock, Inc. Page 58: "Flowers," Odilon Redon: Image courtesy of Corel. Page 59: "Tornado Bahamas," Winslow Homer: Image courtesy of Corel. Page 63: Design for the ceiling of Café Brasserie, Theo van Doesburg: Public domain, http://www.wikipaintings.org/en/theo-van-doesburg/color-design-for-the-ceiling-of-the-cafe-brasserie. Page 69: Design in response to the limits of the natural environment, Mesa Verde, Colorado: Image © Robert Fullerton, 2012. Used under license from Shutterstock, Inc.

171

IMAGE CREDITS

IMAGE CREDITS

Instruments of Design

Page 120: "Studies of a Woman Sleeping," Sir Anthony van Dyck: Image courtesy of Corel. Page 123: "Smoking Scene," William Michael Harnett: Image courtesy of Corel. Page 125: "Children Playing on the Beach," Mary Cassatt: Public domain, http://www.wikipaintings.org/en/mary-cassatt/children-playing-on-the-beach-1884. Page 127: The dot feels even smaller next to the rectangular elements, and conversely the rectangular elements feel even larger next to the dot. Illustration to "Suprematic tale about two squares," El Lissitzky: Public domain, http://www.wikipaintings.org/en/el-lissitzky/illustration-to-suprematic-tale-about-two-squares-1920. Page 129: Pine forest over sea in Greece: Image © Dmitriy Yakovlev, 2012. Used under license from Shutterstock, Inc.; Ruins of temple in Corinth, Greece: Image © Tatiana Popova, 2012. Used under license from Shutterstock, Inc.; Section of the Pantheon by Giovanni Battista Piranesi: Public domain, http://www.wikipaintings.org/en/giovannibattista-piranesi/section-along-the-pantheon-which-showsthe-pronaos-or-portico-and-the-interior-of-the-temple. Page 131: Race road bike: Image © steamroller_blues, 2012. Used under license from Shutterstock, Inc.; Elliptical cross trainer: Image © Dimitar Sotirov, 2012. Used under license from Shutterstock, Inc.; A composition of shapes: "Non-Objective Composition (Suprematism)," Olga Rozanova: Public domain, http://www.wikipaintings.org/en/olga-rozanova/non-objective-composition-suprematism-1. Page 133: A composition of shapes: "Non-Objective Composition (Suprematism)," Olga Rozanova: Public domain, http://www.wikipaintings.org/en/paul-klee/place-signs-1926. Page 138: "Fountain," Marcel Duchamp: Public domain, http://en.wikipedia.org/wiki/File:Duchamp_Fountaine.jpg. Page 143: "Still Life with Letter," William Michael Harnett: Image courtesy of Corel; "Double Goblet," Albrecht Dürer: Public domain, http://www.wikipaintings.org/en/albrecht-durer/double-goblet.

Ethics of Design

Page 153: Stack of wood planks: Image © VladKol, 2012. Used under license from Shutterstock, Inc. Page 157: "An Old Woman Spinning," Nicolaes Maes: Image courtesy of Corel. Page 159: The Bauhaus, Dessau, Germany: Image © c., 2012. Used under license from Shutterstock, Inc.; Captured pechenegs costume design for the opera "Rogneda," Mikhail Vrubel: http://www.wikipaintings.org/en/mikhail-vrubel/captured-pechenegs-costume-design-for-theopera-rogneda-1896. Page 161: Brindle Canyon, Texas topography: Image credit: USGS. Page 162: "Landscape with Peacocks," Paul Gauguin: Image courtesy of Corel. Page 163: "The Golden Screen," James Abbott McNeil Whistler: Image courtesy of Corel; "Pierrot Lunaire," Paul Klee: Public domain, http://www.wikipaintings.org/en/paul-klee/pierrot-lunaire-1924. Page 164: "Le Moulin de la Galette," Auguste Renoir: Image courtesy of Corel. Page 165: "Seine Quays," Paul Cézanne: Image courtesy of Corel; "Basket of Flowers," Jan van Huysum: Image courtesy of Corel. Page 166: "At the End of the Day," Jules Breton: Image courtesy of Corel.

IMAGE CREDITS